HAVE A CUP OF TIBETAN TEA

BY

DAVID B. WOODWARD

xulon PRESS

Have a Cup of Tibetan Tea
by David Woodward

Printed in the United States of America

ISBN 1-594678-00-6

www.xulonpress.com

DEDICATION

To those co-workers and friends with us in Kham,

who contributed so much to our joy.

FOREWORD

❖

I had the luxury of paved roads and daily buses (well, almost!) during several recent trips through the stunning Kham Tibetan region of China's Western Sichuan Province. David and Betty Woodward traveled by horseback! I thought the trip was interminable when it lasted two days longer than we planned, but the Woodwards never even had a plan! I wondered what it must have been like for travelers of an earlier era in the face of unexpected snowstorms, bandits, high rivers or days on end in a tiny mountain cabin.

Beyond logistics of travel through this amazing part of the world, I wondered about the people who inhabited these mountain villages. One glimpse of the beautiful Khambas with the bright red yarn in their hair, flashing long knives at their sides and dazzling turquoise and other stones around their necks, and you can't help ask, what kind of people they were. What would it be like to live as their neighbor? What stories would they tell me if I could understand their language?

David Woodward unveils the mystery in his book *Have a Cup of Tibetan Tea*. He gives us an intimate picture of every day life and ministry among these Tibetan people. He shows us their hospitable nature, their lively sense of humor, a willingness to sacrifice and, most of all, a wonderful responsiveness to the Good News. As the Woodwards tell the fascinating story of their years among the Tibetans, it is heart warming to hear of the opportunities to share Christ that were open to them and their colleagues. We are reminded that today's workers are but adding to a well-built foundation.

As David Woodward relates their story, one cannot help but notice his love and appreciation for the ethnic Han Chinese brothers and sisters who worked along side them. In light of the tremendous barriers that exist between the Chinese and Tibetan cultures, I was touched as I read of the love of Christ that was displayed again and again by Chinese Christians reaching out to their Tibetan friends and neighbors. *Have a Cup of Tibetan Tea* will inspire and encourage today's Chinese Church as they follow their vision of taking the Gospel westward, back to Jerusalem.

The landscape of the life for Tibetans has changed since the days when the Woodwards trekked the mountains to be with the Khamba people they loved. Today, many Tibetans are keen to have the education, technical training, and modern comforts available to others. They are willing to look beyond the traditional way of seeing their world. And, their hearts are more open than ever to the message of Jesus Christ. The Woodwards' story brings us close to the real life of the wonderful Tibetan people. *Have a Cup of Tibetan Tea* provides us with lessons we should always carry in our hearts. They have filled our cup with hope for the future of the Tibetans.

Nancy Sturrock
CAF

PREFACE

by David Woodward

Early westerners in eastern Tibet introduced irrigation, field crops, fruit, and modern education as well as medicine, not neglecting the opportunity to share their upbeat, positive beliefs and joyous relationship with the God they could call "Father". Much of the former was accepted and less of the latter. They were followed by Han Chinese, who enjoyed the same vibrant faith and continue to this day, living lives of self-denial and sacrificial good works among Tibetans. This is not in order to gain merit but to pass on the love of God which they have received in such great measure.

My wife, Betty, and I knew there a little widow with bound feet, who traveled from a coastal province to serve ten years in Tibet, a Chinese official who discarded a secure government job in order to work with Tibetans, a talented book-keeper in the down country city of Chengdu, and a Tibetan who surrendered a Chinese university education in order to return to his people to tell them of the matchless Jesus Christ.

The opportunity facing Tibetans today is to make the

most of what freedoms remain which they can exercise. And there are freedoms they can choose which their parents and grandparents did not have. Some foreigners long to place Tibetans in a time warp with no cultural or artistic variation or change. Meanwhile numbers of Tibetans seek educational and mercantile openings. Ask a Tibetan whether or not he or she would accept the chance for an education in down-country China or abroad and see what the answer would be.

Even fifty years ago many Tibetans sought to travel. Within a week of Betty and I arriving to settle in a Tibetan town regarded as unreached with the Gospel, I was approached enthusiastically by three Tibetan men eager to tell me of their Christian contacts, one in India, another in Gansu, and the third down on the former, less extensive border of Sichuan

We, along with a mixed lot of over thirty others, including twelve Han Chinese, had begun to live and work in eastern Tibet for the sake of those whom we found there. This was prior to the occupation of Tibet. Some Tibetans whom we met were still there when we revisited the area many years later. Some reached India as refugees. In some ways, Tibetans are freer than they used to be. For example, it is easier and quicker for them to travel. Then all over Tibet there is access to radio now including even Christian programming prepared by Tibetans in various dialects. What a change exists now in the diminished financial power of the lamaseries. And the Chinese government has also promoted literacy and schools.

Regarding Tibetans imprisoned during earlier years is an interesting report from Michel Peissel in his book, "The Secret War in Tibet" of the way a Chinese woman "doctor" in a prison camp gained the deep respect of the prisoners by her kindness and protection of those prisoners who were not fit to go back to work. She wore a cross to identify herself as a Christian in spite of heavy criticism from the prison guards and officials. It was her "hospitality" to Tibetan prisoners that reflects the wonderful hospitality of our Savior, whom she knew so well. Her life answered some of the basic concerns of the prisoners. What has been the agenda of the Tibetan Buddhist? It is to seek the answer to these questions: "Who is my friend?" Then, "What's going to happen to me?" And "What shall I do about it?" "How can I be worthy?" And "Who will help me?" She lived out before them the freedom in spirit she had discovered by trusting God's plan of salvation.

Tibetans worldwide are now discovering that Christians among them are not less Tibetan but are rather fulfilled Tibetans. I say worldwide because today there are fifty former residents of Batang, where we once lived in eastern Tibet, now living in New York. What a precious gift they are wherever we meet them, just so we help them find the answer to abundant life.

AN ADDITIONAL WORD

by Betty Woodward

W hen I was eighteen years old, I made what I consider
the most important spiritual transaction of my life.
At the time I was saved and in Bible College and already
heading for overseas ministry. God put before me the claim
he had upon my life: that I was wholly his, but that I must
make a complete surrender of my will in order to make this
effective in my experience.

The words that challenged me then in the Bible were,
"Many are called, but few are chosen" because as the
speaker, to whom I was listening, said, "Few are willing to
be chosen." I went home from that meeting, and that night,
alone in my room, I tried to face what it would mean to be
one hundred percent sold out to God's will, and to make his
will my own.

The one thing that frightened me, and it really did just
that, was the thought of some unknown step or sacrifice that
God might ask me to make in the future on the basis of this
transaction, something that I wouldn't be able to go through.
By the mercy and grace of God I took the step that night in
my heart, and I made a decision, in "cold blood" as it were,

that has affected my whole life. I told God that no matter what he asked me to do, or where he asked me to go, that by his grace and with his help I would obey him. I took his will for mine. Someone has said, "This is the only sure way of always having your own way."

The words of a familiar hymn are running through my head, "Through many dangers, toils, and snares I have already come. 'Tis grace hath brought me safe thus far, and grace will bring me home."

David and I needed grace when we were forced to leave life and work among Tibetans in 1951 after six years filled with joy in what we believed would be our place of service for life. The words of a familiar poem drew us once again to the true goal of our lives – "My goal is God himself – not joy or peace or even blessing, but himself, my God! 'Tis his to lead me there, not mine but his – at any cost, dear Lord, by any road." That road has given us continuous involvement with Tibetans whose lives have been transformed by him.

TABLE OF CONTENTS

CHAPTER 1

ATTACKED BY BANDITS
AT 14,000 FEET

Midway on our first trip by horse in Tibetan country we knew our daily stint traveling across the treeless Litang plain drew to an end. Betty and I wearily concluded this because the sun had already dipped behind the snow peaks to the West. We had quickly found yak caravan men very vague about directions and destinations in this mapless society. The icy winter wind at 14,000 feet beat in our faces, sweeping down from the ranges to the North. Our scarves felt like flimsy gauze.

At last these Washi nomads reached a campsite, and we gratefully slipped down from our saddles. Looking across at the men rapidly unloading their yak, I said to our helper, Phillip, "Let's get the tent up before we build the fire," and gestured at Betty, wrapped in a blanket and standing with her back to the wind. He already had the same idea, and we rushed to unroll the canvas and lift the tall poles while our other helper, Jamba, expertly pounded pegs into the frozen tundra.

The area had plenty of dried yak dung, left by previous caravans, and this traditional fuel can be a lifesaver. But this was winter, and the snow had dampened the dung. Thus, we were glad that we had brought along some charcoal to start fires. However, our choice of a spot in front of the tent, while a bit sheltered from the wind, was unfortunate. The smoke swirled around and blew into the tent, sending us coughing out into the open.

Meanwhile, the nomads with the benefit of goatskin bellows had hot fires going long before we did. We adjusted our tent flaps, and before long we had a bed of coals and less smoke outside. Betty rustled around in the saddle bags for brick tea and food, and Jamba prepared the meal. A full moon came up to lift the gathering darkness. And best of all, the wind fell. Now we could hear the voices of the nomads as they gathered in the animals and pegged them down for the night.

These rugged drivers had started the trip in a surly mood, and we discovered they had been forced to take us by the Chinese military commandant in Litang, our last stop. It was winter, and they argued that their yak needed a rest on the way home. We wondered what we could do, and already Betty's medical help had made a difference in their attitude. We hoped that we would have further opportunity to gain their friendship. And we did.

Suddenly we heard a shout and saw men pointing northward where we could make out a band of horsemen riding in the direction of our camp at high speed. That seemed peculiar, and indeed it was. "Bandits!" came the call, and with that both Phillip and Jamba rushed into our tent and came out with the two rifles they had been carrying for our protection. Colonel Fu in Litang had insisted on supplying us with rifles and ammunition to supplement those that the caravan had. Phillip told the two of us to take cover behind a pile of our loads, which we immediately did, and they went looking for a vantage point from which they could shoot. The dogs in camp began to bark, and then we heard volleys of gunfire from our attackers.

This was met by a rain of shots from our camp, growing in intensity. Then came the sound of pounding hooves as the bandits rode up to the camp, only to veer to the side and pass by. Betty and I could see them for a few moments, and then they disappeared over a rise.

After a little while Phillip and Jamba returned to tell us how they had thrown themselves to the ground behind some hummocks. "We heard some of their bullets hit the ground around us," Jamba said, "There is something different about the sound of their rifles. They are not like ours."

This was confirmed by one of the nomads, who came over to tell us that this was a well-known gang from another tribe. It had been preying on travelers with the advantage of some new and high powered rifles imported from Europe. "They are not Washi, and they better not come back or we'll finish them off," he added.

Next we had a visit from the caravan leaders, Drale and Jitsen, checking us out to be sure that we were all right and not unduly alarmed. "We will have special men on watch tonight," they said, "They won't surprise us again."

"We will be praying that they don't come back," Betty remarked, and they noted her comment with some respect.

In spite of that, the night was somewhat broken by the restlessness around the camp. Before dawn we broke camp, when Jitsen paid us another visit. This time his purpose was to exchange spent cartridge shells for live ammunition, which he knew the colonel had given us. Why should the nomads use their own precious bullets when they had this access to government stores?

I gladly made the exchange and assured him that there were more if the need arose again. He grinned with pleasure, pocketed the cartridges, and strode back to his animals.

That day on the trail we were all grouped closer together. At one point a postal runner met us on his way to Litang, and the nomads briefed him on the bandit attack on the caravan.

Then he came over to talk to Phillip and Jamba since they were fellow townsmen from Batang. "I'll be staying with Dr. Hsiao at his clinic," he told them, "and he'll be happy to know that you defended yourselves so well." This Hsiao Pin-sheng, the doctor in the Litang clinic, was another Bapa or person from Batang. While we had been in Litang, Dr. Hsiao had told us about patients he treated after they had lost an ear, a hand, or a tongue as punishment under tough Tibetan justice.

The postman, Drashi, left us abruptly. We knew he had a grueling schedule, all on foot, fording icy streams, sleeping in caves. "If he rode a horse, traveling alone as he does, it would soon be stolen," Phillip explained.

"Then he wouldn't carry any valuables, would he?" I asked.

"Never!" he replied. "All he has is letters. Valuables go by caravan. That's why we were attacked. And even mailmen are sometimes robbed anyway."

Three days later Postman Drashi caught up with us on his return trip to Batang. Quickly several men gathered around him, eager to hear any news. And what news he had!

We gratefully shared the tea.

20

"Those bandits who attacked you went on to Litang," he announced. "They had the nerve to attack and kill a herdsman in daylight right below the town and drove away his horses. The people were so angry that they pursued the gang and killed two of them. Then they cut off their heads and placed these on stakes up on the main street! The rest of the robbers fled but had to leave the stolen horses behind. The animals were all rounded up. I don't think that gang will ever come this way again."

We urged him to stay on and tell us more, but he still had many miles to travel before he would hole up in a cave for the night. With a wave of his hand he was off and after a while was out of our sight. His postal schedule called for steady, rapid walking, possible exposure to blizzards, as well as danger from wild animals. These runners prized their jobs and took pride in their speed, four days compared to the nine we would take. I remembered Dr. Hsiao telling me that they all made his clinic their headquarters in Litang and with good reason. Sometimes a postman would arrive there utterly exhausted or with pneumonia. "But it is amazing how quickly they are restored to health," he chuckled. "Of course, they place great stock in my medicine and my prayers for them. They insist that I do pray for them, even if they are Buddhists."

When I mentioned this to Betty, she said, "I'm glad that the Hsiaos are praying for us, too. We can use all the prayer we can get. Right now, though, I'm more scared of my horse slipping on the ice than I am of meeting more bandits!"

Who in their right mind would enlist for this kind of boot camp schedule at the top of the world; that is, unless we had some good and compelling reason? And that reason was our conviction that God had been training us for this in our years of preparation at home.

CHAPTER 2

A CLEAR SENSE OF DIRECTION

W ith Betty's father as the candidate secretary of a foreign mission it is not surprising that her attention was drawn early on to the question of whether or not God wanted her to be a missionary. She was very receptive to the idea of going somewhere, and since she had read a lot of Kipling, she hoped that she would land up in India. Nevertheless, she had a sort of nagging feeling that God wanted her in China. "And that is the last place in the world that I would want to go," she told her friends.

But change was in store for her. There came a weekend when she learned that a missionary from China, a Mr. Desmond Guinness, would be speaking at St. Anne's Anglican Church in Toronto where her family worshipped. He would be at evening vespers, and as she thought about it, she decided to settle the China question. "Dear God," she prayed, "I can't stand this uncertainty about China. I'll listen tonight, but if there is no clear word for me, I'll take it that you don't want me in China."

To her surprise, that evening Guinness didn't even

mention China in his message. At the close everyone knelt down on the kneelers for the closing prayer. With a sense of relief Betty was thinking to herself, "Well, that settles that! There is nothing he had to say that would lead me to go to China."

However, right then it was as though she heard God say to her, "Betty, even if you didn't hear anything in that message that would call you to China, that is where I want you." She had never before known anything so unmistakable, and her consternation turned to a quiet, "Yes, Lord, I'll go."

The next evening the church young people had a meeting in the home of the rector, Noel Palmer. The church was having a revival, and as a result the room was packed out. Guinness was there, having stayed over, but it was the rector who spoke on the theme, "Launching Out Into the Deep". When he concluded, Palmer looked at his watch and said, "We have time for a testimony or two. Is there anyone of you who has something fresh to share with us?" Throughout the message the Holy Spirit had been prompting Betty to make a public declaration of her decision of the previous night. This would indeed be cutting the cords and launching into the deep. When no one else ventured to speak, Betty took a breath and began by saying, "God spoke to me last night about going to China."

When she was finished, Palmer smiled and said, "Thank you, Betty, for that good word. I believe that Mr. Guinness here might like to add the other half of the story."

Young people leaned forward with interest. Desmond Guinness was smiling as he said, "Yes, there is another side to what Betty has said. I have felt badly about having to leave my work in China for good, and yesterday morning in another church I poured my heart out in an appeal for young people to consider going to China to spread the Gospel. Not a person responded. I was feeling at a loss in the afternoon, and then I made a proposition to God. I said, "Lord, this evening I'm not going to mention China. I'm not going to make any appeal. But I'm asking you to give me one person in that church this evening to take my place in China. Now I've learned from Betty what God did."

Palmer turned to Betty and said, "And you, because you were willing to share your encounter with God in this public way, you have made it possible for us all to know how God answered his prayer. And you have also had a confirmation of the call of God on your life." Later, as Betty considered where in China she should go, the challenge of reaching Tibet from the China side crystallized.

As for me, my first choice of a place to go was somewhere in Latin America, a place with some similarity to the Spanish heritage of the Philippines, where I was born to missionary parents. When God made it clear to me that he planned for me to go to Tibet, I was startled. I regarded myself as a child of the tropics, and Tibet seemed such a cold and barren land. But I had often sung, "I'll go where you want me to go, dear Lord," and I realized that life was meant to be more than following one's own preferences. I am grateful that my mission emphasized that a true call from God is a call to intimacy, not to a place so much as to loving obedience. And God may lead us first in one direction in order to get us to another goal. Among my friends six other men had declared themselves as ready to go to Tibet, and yet five of them eventually found God had other and eminently useful places of service where he wanted them.

My roommate in college and seminary, Archie Torrey, spent years in Korea, founding Jesus Abbey. Paul Lindell became director of a Lutheran mission, World Mission Prayer League. Fred Renich ministered for years in Missionary Internship. Paul Miller died heroically on the borders of Bhutan. Gordon Gale, a former forest ranger on the Olympic Peninsula, worked for a while in India. And the Swedish missionary, Gus Nordberg, who first drew my attention to Tibet, was himself trapped by World War II in Sweden and then held there by the ill health of his wife. He became a faithful pastor. I had expected to follow in the footsteps of some of these "mighty men" only to find that God had different strategies for all of us. But from each of us he asked obedience.

Let me give you one more illustration of how we were in process prior to our going to Tibet because it will explain how we operated later on. Chattanooga, Tennessee, will always be a special place to me. I had been touring through the southern states with a friend, Wilf Overgaard, speaking on missions in various places. Wilf had mentioned to me that his wife, Evy, was holding back from the thought of spending her life in Thailand. I proposed a bargain to him, saying, "Wilf, I'll pray that Evy will consent wholeheartedly to going along with you to Thailand if you will pray that Betty Gillman will be willing to marry me." He thought that that was a great idea, and so it came about that when we arrived in Chattanooga, he received a letter from his wife. "Praise the Lord!", he said as he read it, and he explained that she was telling him that she had settled the questions she had about going to Thailand and was ready to go.

"Well," I said, "You have gotten the answer to your prayer, and now it must be time for me to get the answer to my prayer." For a year God had kept me in check from expressing my interest to Betty, but here in Chattanooga I got my freedom to do so. So I wrote her in Seattle, and when she received it, she was faced with a conundrum. Her first inclination was to throw my letter in the waste basket, but that posed a problem. The day before that, a young Lutheran pastor headed for Afghanistan had said to her, "Betty, I have a question for you. It is this. Have you ever asked the Lord whether or not he wants you to have a husband as you go to Tibet?"

She bridled at this personal question, but she could see

that he was regarding her in a serious yet kind way. "I know that I can manage perfectly well as a single woman in Tibet," she replied. "When I stated that God had definitely called me to Tibet, the first reaction I got from the mission director was to the effect that I better put a husband at the head of my outfit list. I've never been determined to go out single, but on the other hand I haven't given it much thought."

"You still haven't answered my question," Wilcox persisted. "I was wondering if you have ever asked the Lord just what his plan for you is – to go married or unmarried."

"I can't honestly say that I've ever tackled it that way," Betty replied.

"Well, I suggest that you do," he said, "It is very basic to seek God's will."

That was the end of the conversation, but the next day she couldn't help remembering what he had so recently brought to her mind. My letter was lying on her desk, and she was suddenly sure that she should answer it, guardedly, of course. She typed one carefully worded paragraph and mailed it off to me. I got her letter in Chattanooga, and Wilf and I had quite a party over that. By my third letter I had proposed to her, and she accepted me. Assuredly, God works in mysterious ways!

Our training for the missionary life in those preparatory days had strong emphasis on guided prayer, responsibility for fellow workers, a simple life style, and exercise of faith on the basis of obedience to the Lord. We learned the very big difference between self-reliance and reliance on Jesus Christ. Instead of a short candidate course we had a prolonged period of communal living in our various mission headquarters before we were prepared to go overseas. This was due to the war and the lack of shipping for ordinary travel, but it also gave us special opportunity for getting the solid foundations of faith, hope, and love.

It was in Chattanooga that I received a lesson in balance

that I needed. Wilf and I had some remarkable faith exploits to recount, but after one session a thoughtful, older woman remarked to me, "I note that you both talk a lot about faith, but don't you ever talk about love – compassion – caring?" That admonition was a reminder to speak more about God's chief goals as well as our opportunities for service in his name.

When we finally sailed from Philadelphia, we experienced an outstanding example of love in action. Because it was out of the question to cross the Pacific and get to China in the last days of World War II, we were advised to try the longer route to India where we could study some Tibetan until we could continue on to China. Thus, in March of 1945, we were booked on a Portuguese ship to Lisbon. The day we were to board ship we packed our bags, but there was one hitch. We didn't have the funds to cover our tickets. That morning Betty and I told the Lord, "We're packed and ready, have done all that we can, and we thank you for doing all the rest!" And we waited expectantly.

An hour before we were due to go up the gangway of the ship, the funds arrived. A young missionary candidate sold his beloved red convertible and bought a cheaper car, giving us the difference, and we were on our way. In Lisbon though ships were few and prospective passengers many, we found bookings around Africa and across the Indian Ocean. But in this sellers market the price of tickets suddenly jumped, way beyond the value of our Thomas Cook travel vouchers. Again God took care of us in spite of the price gouging. We had barely enough, but we were able to board our next ship. Then when we landed in India we had only $20 and still the whole country to cross. For the third time God graciously arranged another deliverance for us and the other three members of our party.

But we had an unexpected kind of test ahead of us. Traveling by train in India, we were awakened one night to find the train stopped at a station and a baggage car up front ablaze. We learned later that it had been set afire deliberately in order to hide a robbery. We watched helplessly as our luggage disintegrated, some dinner plates sliding out of a trunk and across the floor of the burning car.

By the next morning's light we saw the charred debris that had been hauled out on the station platform. Our entire outfit was gone except for one small case and two boxes of books, which had been placed in another baggage car. Married three months before, Betty had lost her wedding presents, including many clothes that friends of hers had lovingly sewn for her. All the next day as the train rolled northward in the direction of Bombay we were trying to digest the disaster which had hit us. Betty was thinking, "Why, Lord? We didn't have very much. We weren't able to get everything we might have needed. Why did you take it all away?"

Betty dried her tears and found comfort in some verses she had written in her Bible:

> Let me hold lightly things of this earth,
> Transient treasures – what are they worth?
> Moths can corrupt, rust can decay
> All their bright beauty fades in a day.
>
> Show me thy riches, glory and grace,
> Boundless as time is, endless as space!
> Let me hold lightly things that are mine,
> Lord, thou hast given me all that is thine!

Brave words and true, but we had to live them as well as say them. In Bombay the guest house; where we had booked, was full, and the management arranged for us to stay in a deserted mission residence. From here I tried to make inquiries about our baggage at the railway company offices without success.

Then Betty fell violently ill with malaria and had no appetite for the food I brought her all the way from the railway station. Then when at last she could tease me about having my books spared while she had lost her wedding gifts, I knew she was recovering.

We got past that setback. And by the time we left India for China our mouths were filled with laughter at how God had turned evil into good for us. He had miraculously restored our outfit and better than before, and this from sources within India, chiefly a reimbursement for our loss in the train fire from the railway company. The dire predictions of some old India hands that we would never see any money from the train company had proved false. We were particularly thrilled to be able to purchase needed medical instruments and a good store of medicine very inexpensively from the India Tablet Industry, a mission organization. It packed most of its medicines in recycled tin containers to cut costs. Not very elegant, but they would do well for any clinic we might set up in the eastern Tibet.

CHAPTER 3

BONDING WITH TIBETANS

O ur introduction to life at the Indian hill station of Darjeeling was not in the large houses above the tracks of the D. & H. Railway but in a small wooden bungalow in the scattered Indian and Nepali housing clinging to the hillsides below the tracks. Neither of the houses we lived in there had electricity or plumbing, but the smiles we received from our neighbors gave us a charge. Many a Nepali toiled up the steep paths with a heavy load on his back. In the house on a ledge above us was a Tibetan family, who would call in a red-robed priest from time to time to keep misfortune away with his chants.

We were living in a group of 13, twelve of whom were in language study. Our coworker, Edith Seager, and the two of us were studying Tibetan with a local teacher named Wangden; others were studying Nepali or Urdu. In order to post letters or do a bit of shopping we had to climb up to the main streets of this vacation spot to mingle with tourists, hawkers of souvenirs, insistent Tibetan women intent on renting horses, fruit peddlers, and the occasional member of the British community. One day when I was licking stamps and affixing them to my letters at the post office, an English lady frostily said to me, "You won't last long out here if you keep on doing that." I stopped and I forget what I mumbled to her, but Betty would have heartily agreed with this advice.

After some of our fellow students of Nepali moved out to live in a village near the border of Nepal, Edith, Betty, and I made a move four miles up the ridge to Ghoom, a station on the small gauge railway, and a place where we could meet more Tibetans. We had become acquainted with two elderly Finnish ladies, Misses Tresbeck and Jureva. Since they spent winters in Bombay, we were able to rent their little cottage on the Finnish Compound, a cozy community of Tibetans engaged in a weaving industry. A Finnish couple, the Ollilas, supervised this project, and Mr. Ollila offered to get us Tibetan teachers and also to supervise our studies.

In Ghoom, our alarm clock would go off at five-thirty in the morning, and we had half an hour to get ready for the daily chapel service in Tibetan for the staff and workers. It was dark and frigid, but in minutes the kindling in the stove would be crackling. We always prepared tea in a thermos the evening before and, adding a piece of toast, would have the "little breakfast" or "chota-hausri" like other households around us. That was a great help because the chapel was unheated, the seats and cement floor cold.

My! The greetings as we met each morning were warm, and the singing strong. Because Tibetan has an alphabet which we quickly learned, we could read the text in a hymnbook and sing right out even when we didn't know all the words. Mr. Ollila and the Tibetan evangelist, Tsering, took turns in leading the services. These months as part of a Tibetan congregation were an encouraging experience. And Mr. Ollila began to brief us on the dozen or so Tibetan congregations which had sprung up in the Sikkim, Kalimpong, the border of Bhutan, the western border of Nepal, and in Kashmir. Ghoom itself held memories of the pioneers, like Annie Taylor, or John Fredrikson of the Scandinavian Alliance Mission. On the other hand, it also had a Tibetan temple, serving the resident Tibetans and traders down from Tibet.

We for the first time were gathered with a group of Tibetan Christians. This was a promise of things to come for us, and we were encouraged by their friendliness. The hymnbook we used in Ghoom had been prepared by missionaries in Chinese Tibet, the area for which we were headed. And in these months we actually met a Swedish missionary, David Westborg, who had recently traveled with a Mr. Alfsen, another Swede, in eastern Tibet. They were robbed by bandits of all their possessions traveling between Batang and Derge, towns we had noted on a map. We also met Frank Learner, veteran CIM missionary from northwest China, who opened an inn for Tibetan traders coming into the Chinese city of Lanzhou from the Amdo grasslands and the great Kumbum lamasery. We went to see Len and Iris Moules of our own WEC India-Tibetan field. Len was getting ready for another trip up to the Tibet border, equipped with a movie camera and a notebook filled with scenes which he hoped to film. He would have been glad for us to join them and remain in India, but we explained how strategic and available we felt eastern Tibet to be. The Moules wished us well in these plans and urged us to keep in touch by mail once in China.

When our whole group of language students took some time off and hiked over to Kalimpong and back, stopping at dak bungalows or government lodges on the way, we had the choice privilege of meeting the half-Tibetan, David MacDonald. Now aged, he had known Sadhu Sundar Singh and of his trips into Tibet. MacDonald had served for some years as the British trade agent in Yatung, Tibet, and as a Christian he started a small church there. He showed me an invitation which he had from the Dalai Lama to visit Lhasa, accompanied by a companion. "I was too old to go when this came," he said, and with a twinkle in his eye, added, "I would have enjoyed using this permit and having someone like you to be that companion!" He was so genial and alert that I knew I would have enjoyed such a trip with him, too. I did wonder to myself how many young men over the years had fingered that precious document and wished, as I did, that it could have been used to get into Tibet. It was still forbidden territory for practically all westerners, being independent central Tibet.

Ghoom was often shrouded in mist, particularly in the early mornings when people lined up at the public tap below us to fill their kerosene tins with water. We often watched the crowd down there with great interest. Our young helper, Abel (pronounced with a short "ah"), thoroughly enjoyed the socializing, and we could easily spot him in line by his pink wool cap. In fact, he was very generous in waving others ahead of him if he wasn't through a vital conversation!

When the mists cleared away, we had an incredible view of the five snow-covered peaks of Kanchenjunga across deep valleys, and this contrived to make them seem to be floating in space. And in the winter months they appeared in all their majesty, much more so than in the summer monsoon season. Behind us was a relatively short climb up Tiger Hill to what was regarded as the best vantage point to see Mount Everest. One of the most remarkable scenes in the world is the racing light at sunrise moving along the Himalayan battlements from East to West as far as the eye can see and in just a matter of minutes. The bleak and dangerous snows are transformed as though coming to life. It's a kind of cosmic glow touching God's earth.

Turning to something more mundane but very important, our shift to Ghoom was primarily for the sake of language study. Mr. Ollila was an experienced Tibetan linguist and a recognized government examiner. He also went out of his way to provide us with good Tibetan teachers. Beside our lessons with him we had sessions with the evangelist, Tsering. Then Ollila engaged a scholarly lama or graduate priest, living nearby. He came from the Lhasan nobility and was named Tupchen, but he wore the yellow robes of South East Asian Buddhists instead of deep maroon. "I studied for some years in Colombo, Ceylon," he told us, "and there I was called Umaladassi."

Tsering was a modest and unassuming man with limited education, but he had had years of Bible study. He was gentle and patient with us in class, and he was also helpful correcting our mistakes. He displayed a genuine interest in our progress and was delighted that we were headed for work in eastern Tibet. "You will find some differences in the Tibetan used in Kham," he warned us. "Up in Lhasa the Tibetans from the East do not understand Lhasa Tibetan well, so they live in separate sections of the lamaseries."

On our part we needed to learn conversational Tibetan so that we could communicate. It was embarrassing but also incredibly funny when Betty supplemented her instructions to Abel to get us a bunch of carrots in the market, using some sweeping hand motions. He nodded his head vigorously and hurried off, only to come back later with a skinned cow's tail! Betty despaired of cooking it and told him to take it home to his mother. He was surprised but delighted, and Betty took pains to learn the right word for carrots in Tibetan.

Tupchen was a complete contrast to Tsering. First, in appearance. We could see him coming up the road from a distance with his shaven head and bright yellow robes. But also he was a scholar. He had taught himself to speak flawless English. And he was proud of his own Tibetan language. A born teacher, he handled drills and practice conversation with great skill. I have wondered if he was teaching us less for pay than for what he might observe about us as foreigners. There was a mystery about him which I could not begin to plumb until I visited him in his own rented quarters in an apartment house. To my surprise he had none of the traditional Buddhist worship paraphernalia.

When I pressed Tupchen about his departure from the trappings of Buddhist worship,

he admitted that he was regarded by the local Tibetan priests as an anomaly. "Well, it began when I studied with the Hinayana priests in Ceylon," he said. "They made fun of our Tibetan Buddhist practices and extolled their way as a purer way. I lost my faith in idolatry, and yet I also have a mind of my own. I thought. I meditated. As a result I found that I also had some reservations about my new Buddhist teachers. So now I am neither at home spiritually with my own Tibetan friends or comfortable with the Hinayana sects. I only find peace by myself, and I keep seeking for answers to life's questions. I am an independent guru, and some people here regard me as a holy man. All I can say is that I try to be an honest man."

Gradually he also shared with us his remarkable background in Tibet. He studied at Sera Monastery in Lhasa from age 7 to 20, under the guidance of an uncle who was resident there. "When the Great 13th, the Dalai Lama, died," he told us, "there was an intense political struggle involving the regency which would last through the choice and childhood of the next Dalai Lama.

"Young monks like me were all too eager to be enlisted in the demonstrations and fighting which went on, and I turned out to be on the losing side. Because of that, my family helped me flee my native country. They were so afraid of my danger that they didn't regard India as safe for me. 'No, you must go all the way South to the island of Ceylon or you will be assassinated,' they said to me.

"That was years ago, and those who might have sought my life are no longer in power. Thus, I could go back, and yet I can't. I would be expected to return to Sera and take up where I left off. But at 35 I'm a different man, and I wouldn't fit in. So I travel a lonely road but not unhappy." He smiled, his face the same serene oval as that of the present Dalai Lama.

"He's an intellectual," I thought, "and he's still searching. Satisfied in a way, but not always."

One day I asked him, "And what do you think of us Christians?"

He tapped his knee for a moment and then came up with an answer, "I thought all foreigners were Christians, marked by fighting, drinking, and debauchery. But I know enough now to distinguish between those who follow the teachings of Jesus and those who do not. And there is something different about you Christians. How shall I say it? You are free. The ladies laugh like Tibetan ladies – very open, very happy."

No doubt a good witness to Tupchen would be our diligence to the task at hand. He took studies seriously, and so should we. Thus, we concentrated on preparation for our government examinations and reined in our personal questions of him. As a result Edie, Betty, and I passed the exams without difficulty and thanked our trio of teachers for their excellent help. Tupchen would remain in our prayers as a hungry heart and one whom our Lord thought a great deal about as well.

Moving on to China was now a possibility. It was early in 1946, and its ports were now open. When we wrote inquiring of the manager of the CIM guest house in Chengdu, in west China, about staying there for a period of Chinese study, Mr. Jeffery wrote back welcoming us. "You could go directly there by air," I suggested to Edith Seager, "and we could bring your heavy baggage around with ours by ship."

She agreed to go ahead of us so she sent her passport down to Calcutta for an exit visa. Several weeks went by with no sign of the passport coming back, and her letters on the subject went unanswered. At this point Betty and I decided to go down to Calcutta to see what booking we might get on a ship to Shanghai. We could check on Edie's passport at the same time. When we reached Calcutta, I searched for and found the government passport office. The room I entered was crammed with passports, literally to the ceiling. The official seated behind a desk knew nothing about her application for an exit permit or where her passport might be. "Look around for it," he suggested. Perplexed, I sized up the job I might have before me. Then I reached out for the first handful of passports on a table, saw one that was Canadian, and to my surprise, it was hers and already had both her China visa and the India exit permit. "Here is the Seager passport," I declared, and the functionary hardly lifted his head from his work. "Just take it," he said wearily and didn't ask for any identification on my part! Without comment I pocketed the passport and gladly went my way.

Now that Edie was cleared to leave by plane for China, that left Betty and me to find a ship. Our friends in Darjeeling hadn't held out any hope for us. No ship to Shanghai was in the newspaper listings. Nevertheless, a friendly tip led us to the American consulate and the information that the Chinese community in Calcutta had just been provided a liberty ship which would take 500 Chinese back to China. We immediately applied and were allowed to sail with them on the sturdy but slow moving S.S. James Buchanan. Most nights we slept along with others on the decks in preference on my part to a hold crowded with canvas bunks stacked four high and on Betty's part to a tiny cabin she shared with an American woman, which got the full benefit of the heat from the air vent of the galley! Our Chinese fellow passengers gave us an opportunity to use the limited Chinese we had learned from a fellow passenger on our ship between Lisbon and India the previous year.

This was good for us because we had become so focused on Tibetans that we had failed to think of them in the context of their ancient and modern relationships with their Chinese neighbors. In fact, our year in India had helped us to gain a little understanding of the peoples of India. They interacted to a degree with the hill people and the Tibetans. How kind some of them had been to us; one couple opening their home in Calcutta to us in the last days before we sailed.

And how could I ever forget the kindness I received that night just after we reached India, standing at a ticket window at the train station in Poona. The clerk had told me curtly that there were no compartments available on the next train. I went back perplexed to our party from the boat train, the train which had had the baggage car fire. Now we were exhausted and had missed our connection. Would we have to sit here in this station through the long night hours? It seemed too much to bear. Just then a shipboard acquaintance, Abdul, came up to me, sized up the situation, and then said, "Just wait here. I'll see what I can do." He disappeared through a door and before long came back with the needed tickets, for which I paid him. He then led us to the platform and the right compartment, helped us settle in, and then instructed us, "Lock your door and don't open it for anyone! Other people will try and get in." We thanked him, and he was gone. Sure enough, the pounding at our compartment door continued until the train left. Since we ourselves, with friends, were already twice the number for a compartment for four, we were grateful for Abdul's advice. He was a special "good Samaritan" whom God had sent along at the moment of my despair. How enriched I was by this Muslim like that of other Muslims I had known in my birthplace in the Philippines. Ahead of us would be other valued friends.

CHAPTER 4

MORE TO FOLLOW

W hen I went to a bank in Shanghai to collect a remittance, the clerk behind the counter looked over his list and said, "Your remittance hasn't come yet." I found that hard to believe on the basis of the information I had, so I asked him to let me see his list. It was alphabetical, and I glanced backwards from the W's. Finally I found my name spelled as Aoodward, David B. That mistake hadn't happened before, and it hasn't happened since. Certainly it was not business as usual.

Back at the China Inland Mission where we had been welcomed on our arrival we had been impressed by a large picture in the dining room, a picture of water pouring over Niagara Falls and an inscription with the words, "More to Follow". That picture and its title spoke to us of the steady and adequate flow of God's grace for us on a daily basis and on which we can trust. We needed that encouragement as we set out by ourselves and with very limited Chinese to go up the Yangtze River by steamer to Chungqing in western China. We made the trip relying on help from our very present Lord.

At Chungqing I got off, crossed the river by ferry, and

mounted a steep hill. Then, spotting a phone booth, I went over and began to look for the CIM in the phone book. This wasn't Shanghai, however, and the book had no English listings. It was entirely in Chinese, and I was at a loss. A pleasant gentleman in a long, flowing robe, noting my puzzlement, stepped up and said in English, "May I help you?" And he guided me to my destination, the CIM mission hostel. The Boy Scout lesson I relearned was, "Be prepared!" But I also thanked the Lord for his abundant help. From this city we then traveled by bus to our destination, Chengdu.

When our bus wheezed to a stop outside the massive East Gate of Chengdu, where no one was there to meet us, we gladly collected our bits and pieces and shuffled down the narrow aisle behind other passengers. It was a big step down to the paving stones and a great sense of accomplishment. We had done it, crossing China with much seen and unseen help.

Buses had so many breakdowns that they had no scheduled time of arrival, thus, no one knew exactly when to expect us. We still had to negotiate a trip by rickshaw to our guest house, and we had learned what an appropriate fare would be. With the backing of a fellow passenger I made a deal with a group of rickshaws, and off our procession rolled. The streets of the city at that time were for the most part too narrow to carry motor traffic, and they were full of pedestrians as well. It was hopeless to do any more than trust ourselves to the rickshaw men and settle back. All we knew was that we were heading for the North Gate district.

Our rickshaws finally swung into a gate, and the men lowered their shafts. They were dripping with sweat and began to wipe themselves off. The word of our arrival spread, and our co-worker Edie came out to greet us. "You made it!" she exclaimed. "Come, and we'll get you some tea." I paid off the rickshaw men, and we met the lively couple managing the hostel, Sam and Signe Jeffery. Sam said, "I'll see that your suitcases go up to your room. We have a storeroom down-stairs for the larger pieces." It was a wonderful feeling to be in the hands of such generous efficiency!

Edie started to answer our questions as we walked into the hostel. "There's plenty of room for us to stay on here for several months," she told us. "Missionaries have been leav-ing in large numbers for overdue furloughs, and the new arrivals like us are few and far between. So we're welcome to stay here as long as we require. Of course, it's ideal for language study – no meals to prepare and very quiet! Now how was your trip? And I'm eager to hear the latest news from India, too."

"Well, the most recent thing in our minds is our Yangtze trip," Betty replied, "Every boat we saw going down the river was packed with people returning home to the eastern provinces. And we were surprised in Hankow to find the river bank swarming with demobilized Japanese troops still wait-ing for transport back home!" She stopped for a moment.

"Oh, I've got a pile of mail for you up in my room," interjected Edie.

"How would you like your tea?" Signe asked from the end of the table where we were sitting. Then turning to her two little sons, Bobby and Johnny, beside her, she said, "Yes, you can have two cookies apiece." And we felt like part of a family.

Signe was pleasant and warm-hearted, well-suited to her responsibilities as a hostess. She presided over a small staff, headed by a male cook with a peg leg. Sam was the business manager, tall, soft-spoken, and helpful. At many a mealtime together we listened and picked up useful information about Chinese life and current economic problems. Edie also briefed us, but we three benefited most from Lucille Chang, who had been teaching Chinese to Edie.

"I've had several teachers," Edie told us. "One is a

college student, and she comes here at six in the morning before going to the University. Sometimes I go out to the campus and try out my Chinese on some of the girls there. But the teacher I like best is Lucille. She knows about your coming and is willing to teach us three as a class. Oh, I should warn you. None of these friends will accept any payment for teaching. They say, "We realize that you have come all the way from your home and are willing to go to hard places, places we Chinese should be responsible for. So it is as little as we can do to give you some time teaching you our difficult language."

"After our trip across China, we're convinced that we need more Chinese," I said, "We won't always have the help of a friend to speak for us. But neither do we want to lose out on our Tibetan by being away from speaking it for too long."

"For right now, I find this comfortable house and lovely garden most enticing," Betty remarked with a laugh. "The way I feel right now I may not be able to tear myself away!"

"Yes," Edie answered, "and look at what a short time I have been here and already I am attached to the college students as well as my class of middle school boys. I could easily swing into a very rewarding work with them. That's what some of the missionaries I've met tell me – that a lot people intending to go to Tibet find such a response among the Chinese that they stay down here."

"But we've already had a sampling of Tibetan life," I added. "Enough to want more."

Our class with Lucille soon began. She came over in the afternoons after her work as an accountant was done at the Canadian Mission Press. A slip of a woman, her hair smoothly combed back and wrapped in a bun, she had luminous eyes that impressed us immediately as showing deep intelligence. We quickly learned that she was not a native Sichuanese, that she had lived in eastern China in the home of a Dr. and Mrs. James Graham, during high school and college. Born himself in China, Dr. Graham was an educator who evidently had great rapport with students. The result of the Grahams' hospitality to Lucille was that she felt completely at ease with westerners.

Later she married a business man, who was away from home most of the time. And they had a teenage daughter, Anna Louise. After Lucille volunteered to teach all three of us, the Jefferys invited Lucille and Anna Louise to move into the hostel, which they did. This arrangement was a great convenience all around and increased our opportunity to learn Chinese, including field trips with Lucille around the city. On the Silk Street, we asked a clerk, "Do you export any of your silks to Tibet?" "Oh, yes," he said, "There are special factories producing sashes, silk braid for the hair, silk for blouses, and brocade for robes. We provide brighter colors for the Tibetan trade."

Lucille observed, "It's an ancient trade we have with Tibet. Thirteen hundred years ago during the Tang Dynasty a market was set up in Kangding to buy horses and wool from the Tibetans in exchange for our tea and silk. We get a lot of furs and medicinal herbs from there as well."

Not long after we started our Chinese classes Betty began to experience severe migraine headaches, similar to some she had ever since arriving in China. She checked with foreign doctors in the city, but they were not able to trace the source of the problem. We decided that this was a definite satanic attack on her ability to continue language study. One evening Edie, Betty, and I made this a definite matter for united prayer, and immediately the headaches ended, much to our delight.

Betty and I had a constant reminder of Chengdu's antiquity by the old city wall where we took daily walks in the cool of the evening. It was close by, but to get there we jostled through narrow lanes, frequently being passed by the "honey bucket" brigade, taking human ordure out to spread on the fields outside the city.

We would mount the steps of the city wall with relief, stroll on its broad top, and on clear days we could even spot the snow peaks of Tibet to the West. They seemed more of a reality, and not a backdrop, when at last we had a visit from our first Tibetan from the China side of Tibet. He was from Batang, 200 miles into the Tibetan province of Kham or what was called the Chinese province of Sikang. Phillip, as he spelled his name, was a young man who had been sponsored for schooling by a lone missionary nurse in Batang, Gladys Schwake. Currently he was trying to gain entry into a junior college and working meanwhile in a Chengdu hospital as an aide. He beamed innocently at the sight of us with his broad, open face and a boyish smile. Right away he was a booster for his home town, saying. "Why don't you come to Batang? There's no place to compare with it in all of eastern Tibet. This time of the year the fruit is ripening – apples, apricots, peaches – and the first crop of grain is ready for harvest! We have two harvests every year in Batang valley!" He spoke freely in English, but we were also able to try out our limited Tibetan on him. Phillip immediately began to explain some of the dialectal differences between Lhasa and Batang to us. We later learned that in his childhood for safety his parents had named him with the name of a god and with a female name, both of which Phillip had been eager to discard once in school.

Phillip entered our circle so rapidly that big-hearted Sam and Signe included him in a summer vacation party going to the river city of Guanxien. Two thousand years ago the waters of the Min River were divided there in a complex irrigation system for the whole plain. Guanxien was famous all over China for this achievement. So we were in high spirits as we boarded the bus – among us also Lucille, Anna Louise, and "Peg-leg", the cook. He was the last one to board, and the door slammed shut on his wooden leg. No harm done, of course and he finally hoisted it inside! When we reached Guanxien, it was already lunchtime, so Signe called out, "It's too late to prepare lunch ourselves, so we'll just eat on the street."

"Eat on the street!" exclaimed Betty, taking her literally.

"Oh, that's a Chinese expression for eating at a restaurant," Signe hastily enlightened her.

That evening there was a knock on our door, and Lucille came in with a bowl of what looked like white dumplings, and some chopsticks. "This is your share of 'tang-erh'," she said, handing them over and rushing off. "What is this?" I asked Betty.

"I don't know, Watch out; they're hot!" Betty said. We lifted our chopsticks slowly. Lucille had never failed us before, but this looked very plain and sticky. What was it? How would it taste? We each lifted one of the round balls and held it, blowing on it. Finally we each tried a tang-erh, not chewing, just rolling it around. Mine seemed so tasteless that I turned to spit it out, but Betty made dire signals to me that I must not fail this test. I gulped, and the rice flour ball went down. Then I pointed at Betty and insisted that she do the same. Which she did, and we collapsed with laughter. "Lucille will come back and want to know how we liked them," I said, "and what will we tell her?" It wasn't until we bit into the next ones that we found that each dumpling had a center of sugar and sesame seed and tasted delicious. After that we finished the whole bowl of these delicacies and could honestly thank our teacher for bringing in this treat.

Much refreshed by the summer break, we returned to our studies. In the early fall we were surprised to receive a letter from Miss Schwake in Batang. Likely she had heard of us through Phillip. Anyway, she was inviting us to come to Batang, deep in Tibetan country and near the political border of Lhasa-controlled Tibet. She wrote,

"It is over a year now since my fellow worker, Mr.

Nichols, followed his family and left here. His heart had been acting up so badly, I was relieved to see him go. He was really a sick man, and I worried about him until I heard that he had reached Kangding.

"I keep busy with the clinic, the care of the compound, church services, letter writing, and the several children I keep in my home – but I do get lonely sometimes for a foreigner to talk with. If you folk would like to come out here, I could fix up space for you to live in the hospital building."

This suggestion went far beyond anything we had been considering. Up to this time we had been expecting to move soon to Kangding on the old Tibetan border. While in Chungqing we had met George Kraft of the CIM, who lived in Kangding. He told us of some Chinese missionaries going there soon for language study and indicated that he would be willing to assist us also with getting Tibetan teachers. Kangding seemed like a logical place to study and then from which to explore into Tibetan country. With our trip across China fresh in our minds, we questioned if we wanted to move on beyond Kangding and undertake the long, rugged trip by horse to Batang. The factor which kept it a live option was the thought of Miss Schwake, who had been out there on her own for over a year. We suspected that we might face dangers on such a journey, yet we could not bring ourselves to write Gladys and tell her it was out of the question for us to come.

Those days in Chengdu we often saw another Gladys at the guest house –Gladys Alyward, the "Small Woman" who came out from England on the Siberian Railway. She was an independent missionary, who had developed a reputation as a vibrant and fearless person. Living as she did in a single room at a church, she appreciated the opportunity to come over at the invitation of the Jefferys in order to wash her hair. Drying her hair on the front porch, she would tell us story after story of her remarkable life in China. Her comment about our chance to go to Batang was, "I'd jump at it!" Phillip pushed us closer to a decision by coming in one day, full of excitement, to tell us that a Tibetan air force bomber pilot, who was from Batang, had reached Chengdu on his way on home leave. Gesang had been away from Batang for ten years, including two years spent in training in the United States. When we met Gesang, he urged us to accompany him. "I'm going on to Kangding, but I'll wait there for Colonel Fu, the Kham area military commander," he said. "By the way, Colonel Fu is down here in Chengdu right now. Would you like to meet him?"

We hesitated because matters were developing faster than we could take in. But in a day or so we received an official red invitation card for a feast at the Colonel's residence. We remembered a comment Gesang had made, "Colonel Fu is especially interested in foreigners because of all the unusual foreign things they bring with them." It would be discourteous to refuse to go, but just where would this lead us?

The evening of the feast Betty, Edie, and I rolled up to Colonel Fu's gate in rickshaws. The guards admitted us, and we strolled up through the garden to a pavilion where the tables were set. The mysterious Colonel Fu met us cordially and insisted that we were the special guests of the evening. Tall, thin, and with a hawk-like face, he was the perfect host, but he soon got down to business. Nothing would do but that we travel with him to Batang, as it was the only way to insure our safety. He could arrange the transport. We would all start the next week!

It was an exhausting evening because Colonel Fu all along acted as though this was a "fait accompli." We had a delicious nine-course meal. Colonel Fu regaled us with stories about battles he had engaged in around Batang and Litang. He stressed the death of Dr. Shelton in Batang after a gunshot wound received from a bandit. Then he pressed us to agree to accompany him, and we barely managed to keep from committing ourselves. Back at home we struggled with what graceful way we could find of excusing ourselves from the good offices of Colonel Fu. We didn't want to be under heavy obligation to him, believing that too close an association might handicap us in developing friendships with Tibetans. We didn't want to offend this powerful man, but somehow we had to maintain our neutrality from the beginning of our life in eastern Tibet.

Actually we found a very simple solution which even Colonel Fu could understand. A remittance we had been expecting from the States had not come through, and we did not have enough money in hand to cover the expense of moving ourselves in as far as Batang. I didn't need to spell out the details, but I sent a message to him thanking him for his kind offer, explaining that we had some unfinished business we had to take care of. He understood and accepted that as a commonplace occurrence. Perhaps his offer was just a gesture of courtesy in case we really were ready to move into Tibetan country.

A growing concern which we had was the matter of finding someone in Chengdu who would handle our business affairs in money exchange and the purchasing and shipping of trade goods to us. We anticipated some of our own reinforcements within a year, but we did not compare with larger missions who could assign their own support staff to business matters. We didn't discuss our thoughts on this subject with others but continued to pray about it.

Gladys Schwake wrote us again, offering to arrange for Phillip to accompany us on the trails to Batang if we decided to come. This would, of course, give us a capable companion. Now if we could find ourselves a business agent to handle sporadic details, we wouldn't have to be a burden on a larger mission.

Then one day our teacher Lucille mentioned that the Lord had been telling her to offer her help with our down-country business. "But you have already done so much for us!" came to our lips.

"Yes," she replied, "and every bit of it has been a pleasure. I have been thinking about your situation when you get way off into some far away place without banks or stores, and it is obvious to me that I'm well fitted to help you with your business from time to time. I know the value of things and how to strike a bargain. Let me do this for you as my way of having a part in reaching Tibetans with the Gospel."

We were touched; how we were touched! Here was another evidence of the special sense of responsibility that Chinese Christians have for the minority peoples to the West of them. Edie had talked to one teacher who had a number of students getting ready to go to Tibet, some of them Chinese, and even Tibetans, who had come down to the plains for advanced studies. Now here was Lucille willing to make a sacrifice in her busy life for our sake. She was already very active with Inter-Varsity Fellowship, and she would be adding one more commitment. We looked at Lucille and couldn't refuse her. She looked too calm and confident about the matter.

So we wired Gladys that we would be coming. Phillip had already moved up to Kangding and was waiting there for us. When we three finally left Chengdu at the end of October, 1946, on the six-day trek we were on our own once again, this time with more Chinese language but still woefully inexperienced. The first day we traveled by truck on the Chengdu plain toward the western foothills. The road was cluttered with foot traffic, mostly men with baskets of produce on carrying poles over their shoulders. Heavier loads were pulled and pushed on rubber-tired carts. The fields still had some late crops, and bamboo groves and trees kept things green. The farmhouses for the most part had gray tile roofs and white stucco walls. Shop fronts along the way had been splattered with mud: red, sticky Sichuan clay.

We began to climb into the foothills and dip into valleys.

Then we commenced a new form of travel, using "chairs" carried by porters, and heading up the tea road into Tibet. The chairs were not enclosed. They were made of a sagging row of bamboo slats for seating between two long bamboo poles, as well as a strip of cloth sunshade hoisted about two feet above the contraption. For a heavier person the carriers on the poles at the front and behind had a third relief carrier taking turns with them. The tea carriers we passed had no such relief, bent beneath loads that sometimes weighed over three hundred pounds. Frequently they had to stop, and for this they carried a stick to place under their load, taking the weight off their back briefly. These carriers brought the brick tea, so desired by Tibetans, from the hot plains up to Kangding's elevation of 8,000 feet, where yak caravans would assume the burdens. Yak could not survive if they went down farther into the heat at low altitudes. Our heavy baggage had been shipped ahead of us, but we also had some porters carrying loads.

We enjoyed the fresh air, the rushing streams, the mountain vegetation – ferns, vines, and shrubs. The main crop on the hills had been corn, and much of this was now drying on racks in front of the huts we passed. I often walked rather than ride in my "chair" because I wanted the freedom to stretch my legs and examine the passing scene more closely.

The inns along the way provided small rooms, wooden beds, but also, wonder of all wonders, small tubs of hot water for our feet! This, and cups of refreshing tea! What matter the mud floor or the rickety table where we ate a meal, or the dogs underneath, hunting for scraps? At least we had spray cans to exterminate the bedbugs, and no amount of scuttling rats would interfere with our sleep.

We were entering country which had at one time belonged to Tibetans, but by now they had been pushed back to higher elevations by Chinese settlers. Yet some of them still came down for trade. I met a group of Tibetans striding down the road with their felt hats, wool robes, and leather boots. I greeted them, "Friends, how are you?" They lighted up immediately and broke into grins at being addressed in Tibetan. "We're fine. Are you tired?" They asked. "Not tired," I answered. "Where are you going?" "We go to Yaan to buy tea and salt. And you, where are you going?"

"To Batang."

They took a double-take, expecting me to say Kangding. Then one said, "It's a long way. Go slowly!" And I replied. "Go slowly!"

We were climbing up to a 10,000-foot pass, so the going was getting slow. As we reached the top, the majestic white peaks around Minya Gonka, the tallest peak in the region, broke into view across the river valley below us. The air was chilly, and each step was taking us closer to the land of our dreams. We had arrived at the doorstep and would soon enter in.

Our porters with the luggage dragged in after dark, one by one. In the flickering light of a candle we paid them out extra "meat money" as compensation for the hard climb.

Lucille back in Chengdu had played the vital part in getting us on this tea road into Tibet. And she would continue to help us for the next five years, cheerful and consistent. She was a faithful partner and a constant inspiration to us. She had shown us that Chinese Christians did not call the Tibetans barbarians and could see their potential as people God loves.

The next day, our last, we were surrounded by steep mountain cliffs and deafened by turbulent torrents. We followed the Tung River until we reached a smaller tributary leading up to Kangding. The city is located in such a confluence of narrow clefts in the mountains, the joining of two wild rivers, that it is easily defended. In the 1930's the Chinese Communists on their Long March were unable to capture this center though they did take Luding below it. The Chinese Nationalist military in control did finally subject the Tibetan royal house of Chala in Kangding. Monasteries and Tibetan caravansaries vied with modern government buildings and Chinese store fronts for space. The Chinese government had harnessed water power for electricity, and the lights excelled that of Chengdu, where several nights a week we had had to use small oil lamps.

Phillip, by this time in the city, greeted us enthusiastically. He hastened to brief us, telling us that Gesang had left with Colonel Fu's caravan several weeks before. "But I know of a good caravan of traders that will soon be leaving," he added.

In the days of preparation that followed Betty and I thought frequently of the missionaries who had come and gone from Kangding over the previous 75 years such as Polhill, Rijnheart, Shelton, Edgar, and Cunningham to mention a few. And before them the cobbled streets had echoed for centuries with travelers heading for or arriving from Lhasa.

CHAPTER 5

RISK TAKING FOR A PURPOSE

I'm going to describe the border city of Kangding in later chapters. At this point it was a delightful way station where we received warm hospitality from CIM missionaries, had our loads prepared for the road, and secured a caravan headed westward toward Batang.

In one respect we had a major change of plans. When CIM workers George Kraft, whom Betty and I had first met in Chungqing, and Ed Beatty learned from us that we intended to go through to Batang, they advised strongly against this. The tall, soft-spoken American and the genial Englishman were obviously concerned for our safety although various coworkers of Miss Schwake had in the past made this trip.

We three then reviewed our strategy in view of one new piece of information – that a Lutheran lady missionary, Margaret Miller, was soon coming to Kangding and would likely welcome sharing a house with Edie Seager. A suitable building was available right next to the CIM compound. The question was – should we take the house and leave Edie in

Kangding for language study while Betty and I continued on to Batang. Our plan then would be to return to Kangding the following year when we expected two more co-workers would arrive. Edie said she was willing to stay and moved into the new housing. Then the two of us finished last preparations for our trip to Batang to help Miss Schwake.

The day we left.

The day we left we rode for several hours out to the first stage, a small place called Jeddo. Our party of four consisted of Phillip and another Batang student named Jamba, Betty, and myself. Other travelers and the load animals were due there later in the day. We checked into a dilapidated inn, well below Jeddo Pass. It was a wooded area with scattered plumes of steam from hot springs. Betty rested while I decided to locate the nearest hot spring. After a Tibetan pointed me up the hillside behind the inn, I found it easily. There I lolled by myself in a natural hot tub, amid the rising steam. In clear view out across the valleys I had a majestic panorama of the snow peaks around Kangding. Suddenly a flurry of snowflakes started falling around me! Snowflakes and steam – what a combination, but not surprising for November. Refreshed, I then returned to the inn. There Betty was guiding Phillip and Jamba in our first supper, using one of the community stoves.

These clay structures had no chimneys but three-pointed vents where large iron pans fit. The wood fires created an increasing amount of smoke in the kitchen area, and in fact, throughout the building. Our only escape was to crouch low down as close to the floor as possible. Then, supper over, we four turned in, only to be wakened later on by the arrival of our fellow travelers from Kangding. These merchants were in such high spirits that they took two hours to settle down. The wake-up call came at 3:30 in the morning, and everybody began to stir at once. Breakfast was catch as catch can with tea and roasted barley flour. We left around five a.m. with the merchants assuring us that the yak drivers with the load animals were already ahead of us. As we rode along the rocky trail the other riders were dim, silent shadows, but when the grey dawn arrived, the men began to talk and sing. We were climbing continuously, weaving back and forth around huge granite boulders. Near the 14,000 foot pass we were suddenly enveloped in heavy mist. Then as we groped along, we heard the sound of running feet. The men nearest us whispered, "Bandits," and fanned out for cover. Before we could dismount, we heard several shots fired. As we stared into the mist we got a brief glimpse of figures racing for cover and disappearing below us. Our party reassembled and agreed that the danger was past, but we would proceed with care. No more singing or talking after that the rest of the way to the top, the only sounds being the clump of hooves and panting of horses as they labored their way up. The animals stopped from time to time. Then at last we heard some shouts a short way above us, and we knew some of the men had reached the pass. A few minutes later we could see Jeddo La.

The top was marked by the traditional pile of rocks surmounted by prayer flags. These cloth strips glistened with hoarfrost, but not far below us lay the grasslands, dry and brown with only a few snow drifts. The slope down to them was covered with light snow, but the sky above was now a bright blue. Scrub bushes dotted the landscape. It didn't take us long to get down to the flat valley we would follow. It was an empty but open area, still untouched by the rising sun. Betty turned in her saddle and said to me, "At last we're in Minya country." She pointed ahead where the first Tibetan farmhouse was in sight, saying, "This is Tibet for real!" After a while we passed our drivers and the load animals. When the merchants decided it was time for a tea break, they stopped and lit some hastily gathered brushwood, brought water from a stream, and boiled up the rough tea leaves with the help of a goatskin bellows applied to their fire. We gratefully shared the tea, wiped a few drops from our wooden bowls and then tucked them away. We had some hours to ride before our lead riders turned in to the right toward another farmhouse. Phillip grinned as he announced, "That's where we're going to stop for tonight."

We clattered over a bridge in front of the place, and dismounted stiffly. The structure looked like a medieval castle, a sturdy, black fortress with only narrow slits for windows at the upper levels. The stream we crossed to enter made me think of a medieval moat. Now what would it be like inside the massive wooden doors?

Walking our horses in, we reached a crowded and dirty stable area. The watchdogs tied at one side were in frenzy, and we skirted around them in the semi-darkness to where a notched pole reached up to the second floor. Phillip practically scampered up this, carrying Betty's saddle bags, and then stood at the top as though saying, "See, Mom; no hands!" Jamba followed him with equal agility, taking my saddle bags. In contrast we edged up slowly, notch by notch, clinging to the pole to keep our balance. By the time we reached the top, there was Phillip above us, beckoning from the third and top floor. We reached that after a climb on another notched pole to find that he had secured the family chapel as quarters for Betty and myself. Usually reserved for any resident or visiting priests, the chapel had an altar, gilt images, butter lamps, and Tibetan scriptures wrapped tightly in cloth. "You can sleep here," he told us, directing our attention to two wooden platforms, covered with beautiful rugs. "This is really great," I replied. "We weren't expecting anything better than the boards we had last night." When he disappeared, we laid out our sleeping bags and had a nap. Later Betty had two patients, two of our companions who had taken a spill racing on their horses. They proudly showed off their bruises and cuts, and she fixed them up. Then we had a snack, sitting by the small charcoal brazier between our "beds", drinking tea, and trying to adjust ourselves to this ornate apartment. Later we looked out the doorway and noticed a woman as she conducted an evening ceremony of burning juniper in a corner stove. She chanted prayers with palms lifted up together. There was no doubt in our minds that she took this duty seriously.

We had seen pictures like this, but now we were witness to Tibetan family worship practice in its home surroundings. In a matter of hours we had crossed a mountain barrier and had become a part of this alpine land, which was so starkly different from bustling China. It was like going through the looking glass. Oh, yes, we had visualized this, but the impact of unspoiled Tibetan life as it had been for ages was enormous. Here was a culture in which the woman whom we were observing was totally at home while we were the outsiders trying to understand how she felt and what she might be thinking. We could adopt new life styles, like notched poles and wooden bed platforms. We would need to cope with smoke-filled kitchens. But when it came to this type of worship, we sensed something totally foreign to our own personal relationship with God. We felt sad at the rote repetitions we were hearing even while we respected the woman's dignity and devotion.

The following morning we riders didn't start until 8:30 although once again the slow yak caravan had gone much earlier. The trail for the day wound along between brown, rounded hills. The fields in the valley had been harvested of their peas, barley, oats, and turnips. The flat roofs of the farmhouses were crowned with stacks of barley. About ten o'clock in the morning we were passing an inconspicuous sod house. Phillip hailed the farmer standing in the door-way, and to his delight found that the man was himself from Batang. Phillip identified himself as a "Bapa", and the man then insisted we stop for tea. This call on his part for us to "rest awhile" would be so he could get the latest news of Batang people, Batang people in Kangding were a close knit community. Contacting them going and coming was one of the advantages he had by living so close to the trail. His wife poured boiling tea into her churn, added salt and butter, and churned furiously. The result was tasty butter tea, and we drank cups of this. Next, she put some tsamba flour in our bowls which we moistened with tea and ate. Such hospitality, based largely on those wonderful hometown ties! Jamba and Phillip chatted away with the couple, and then we parted to catch up with our caravan.

I noticed that Betty's horse began to lag, and when I asked her what the problem was, she said with disgust, "This horse is a nibbler! He started eating back there when we stopped. Now he keeps munching grass and pays no attention when I pull on the reins. He must have an iron mouth." This last had a note of desperation. Noting her difficulty with the horse, Jamba jumped down and broke off a small branch and handed it to her to use as a switch. With this in hand, Betty managed to urge her horse on its way, but it was still quite a job. Phillip tried to console her by saying, "We'll change our riding animals at our next stop. This is the last time you'll need to ride that horse."

Collecting new riding animals at our stop, Dungolo, took a day's layover because it involved fresh "ula" transport, a government-arranged system of forced supply of animals to travelers for this service. It was a type of taxation on farmers and avoided travelers getting stranded. They did pay a modest amount to the local farmers.

While waiting for the new animals to arrive, we wandered around looking at the ruins of an old watchtower such as originally stood at every stage between Kangding and Fish River, the Tibetan "Nya Chu" where we were headed. This one was still impressive, standing tall as it did against the skyline.

We woke up our second day at Dungolo, to find a foot of fresh-fallen snow, and knew that meant trouble on the high pass we were due to cross that day. "The horses must stay behind the yak today," Phillip told us, "They can't break through such deep snow. Only the yaks are surefooted and strong enough to do that. So we'll have to move along at yak pace." How true that turned out to be, and after five minutes in the saddle we had new appreciation of the yak in our caravan.

"That sheepskin-lined jacket I got made for you should prove its worth today," Betty told me. From our saddles we were watching the procession of loaded yak move patiently forward like snowplows, using their strong legs and heavy chests and shoulders. They kept moving slow and steady, and we had to accept that. When the sun came out, the glare on the snow was blinding. Our sunglasses didn't help much. The yak drivers began covering their eyes with hair, either their own long hair or if cropped, using some yak hair to squint through.

It was a taxing climb to 15,400 feet and then instead of making a descent we remained up on a snowy plateau. The snow was soft, and our horses kept falling to their knees and picking themselves up. "They're only shod on two feet if at all," Phillip explained, "and that's not enough to grip in this kind of snow." When we weren't busy keeping our grip on our saddles, our eyes could rove over the most majestic sight we had ever seen – rows and rows of snow peaks like the waves of the sea. We had a view of them for some 300 degrees around us. From here one missionary had counted 125 peaks. That, of course, was in summer. We wouldn't be counting peaks this bitter day in November!

As the wind howled around us, we felt as if we were gradually becoming permanent parts of the frigid scene surrounding us. Betty wound a white "kata" or ceremonial scarf, around her face to protect it. By this time we were yearning to get off the exposed mountain top, but we had no choice but to plod along. We simply endured until at last we rounded over a second pass and started down, chased by the wind. Betty's horse began to run, and she tried to slow it down. What a sight she was, her horse, belly-deep in snow, its forelegs much lower than its hind legs, and Betty clutching the pommel of her western saddle. Just then two pack mules shoved by her, making her position on an edge even more precarious. After that scare she was all the more ready to dismount even though we had to lead our horses down a stream bed of jagged rocks and pools of water. When we reached a valley below, it was still so deep in snow that we remounted, our horses slipping and stumbling from fatigue. We had been going steadily for eight hours before we gratefully reached a squalid hamlet.

Phillip and Jamba, ever helpful, were quickly on the lookout for a place for us to sleep and found us a side shed. The landlady drove out the pigs and chickens. From somewhere the young men found two doors, placed them on trestles, and proudly led us to our beds for the night. We thanked them as we sank down on the hard planks. It was too cold for bedbugs such as infested Chinese inns, so we could count our blessings in these very bleak circumstances.

The next day we were still forced to follow the yak down through a narrow valley. This was no paved highway. The so-called "trail" was an undefined area filled with boulders and broken rocks. When a horse skated on the ice and crashed down, the other riders waited for a moment to see if the rider was hurt. If he rose off his fallen animal, they began to joke and laugh at him. Thus we went along, threading our way through heavy forests of fir and pine. Some of the trees were extremely tall. Our companions were mostly young, happy to be on the open road and heading toward home, always ready to break the tedium by starting into yodeling at the top of their lungs.

About noon that day we travelers stopped to rest in a house along the way. We were all gathered in a room on the second floor, sipping tea and crunching snacks, when suddenly there was a deafening explosion. Our heads swiveled around to see Phillip pointing a rifle toward a window and looking very embarrassed. Then our attention shifted from him as soot began dropping down on us from the blackened beams above, the collection of years landing all over our clothes.

We had no protection from this soot, and it was so greasy that we couldn't wipe it off. What a mess! It looked like we would have traces of this incident for some time to come. What did our fun-loving Phillip think he was doing?

He tried to explain himself above a chorus of voices. "I picked up Pasang's rifle and pointed it at him. He didn't like that, so then I placed it on his shoulder and aimed it out the window. I pressed the trigger, assuming the rifle was unloaded. And it went off! I didn't mean to shoot." Pasang angrily replied, "Look where the bullet splintered the window frame. You can't even shoot straight!" He had thought at first that his ear had been hit, and he certainly had been deafened. That's why he was furious. The others calmed him down and tried to make a joke of it. But he was still grumbling. We could see that Phillip was shaken. Later he confided in us, saying, "Pasang belongs to Banda Tsang, the biggest merchant family in Kham. If he had been injured or killed, the whole of Banda Tsang's men would go after me."

"And who or what is Banda?" I asked.

"The Banda family is led by three brothers, and they can raise an army," he told us. "Nobody wants to cross them, and everybody respects them." He looked across at Pasang. "And their men are very proud of that. They feel powerful, too."

As we got back on the road he was still trying to explain himself. "I saw a triangular rock outside the window, and I said to myself, 'If that were a rabbit . . .' and pressed the trigger. I was as surprised as anybody at what happened next!" And he laughed, and we laughed. But I think our laughter and his were due to relief at his narrow escape.

"Somebody has been praying for Phillip," I said to Betty, and she replied, "I pray for him and Jamba every day, just like I pray for us and our horses." It helped to laugh and forget the precipitous slopes and the raging torrents below us. That water would reach the Fish River long before we did.

It was 5 p.m, a long day in the saddle, when we wearily heard the welcome roar of a river. Soon we saw Yachiang, a cluster of houses and narrow streets looking a little like some of the forts we had seen in movies of the French Foreign Legion, minus the desert, of course. We were well ahead of the load animals, so by the time they arrived we had found an upstairs room and I watched out the window at the unloading below. The drivers handled it all with dispatch. Supporting a box on a raised knee, a man would loosen the knot in the leather ties, and then carry the load away from the yak at a run as the thongs came loose. An animal carried from 120 to 160 pounds, but we had one box that alone weighed over a hundred pounds. That required a balance of weight on the other side and the strongest beast in the herd.

Waiting five days in Yajiang for fresh animals gave us a good rest although Betty found that she had a number of patients daily. We were there long enough to see some of them respond to treatment. Application of a sulpha ointment on sores worked wonders and made her patients more willing to follow instructions. Betty would supply them with two bandages, torn up from old sheets. When it was time for a change, the patient could use the spare and wash the soiled one. That was the best she could provide with our available supplies, and this system was easier for the Tibetans to follow. In any case, it would not make sense to them to throw anything as prized as cloth away.

In their sheepskins or gray woolen robes onlookers crowded the doorway of our room, vitally interest in listening to the symptoms and diagnosis being described. Betty was puzzled by the physical complaints of one obviously healthy man until she found out that actually he was trying to mimic his mother's symptoms, and this woman lived two days' travel away! Betty hoped that the antacid she gave the son for her would give the woman some relief.

We had not anticipated the flow of potatoes, eggs, turnips, meat and live chickens which grateful patients would bring us. Since we had exchanged gifts with local Chinese officials, we also received a chicken and 23 eggs from one of them and a leg of mutton from another. The mayor came and asked Betty to visit his wife because she was in great pain. As Betty climbed up the notched pole in his living quarters and then saw that the mayor's wife was very pregnant, she happily provided her with a supply of "green" pills, which were baking soda for her heartburn. That solved the young woman's discomfort quickly.

Between times we went for walks, mostly along the river bank, threading our way past boulders and sometimes sitting on a flat one. As we watched the roiling waters, we realized that we would have to cross them next. Betty talked frankly about her having been exhausted on the trip, but she smiled wryly as she told me, "I can't bear to think of retracting our steps over the horrible country we've covered, so we might as well go on. Surely it can't be much worse than what we've already been through."

The day came for us to move on, and we packed our saddle-bags. Just then Betty was interrupted with an emergency case. A young girl, who had been carrying a load of wood down the mountainside, fell, and was carried in with a bad gash on her knee. It needed suturing, but all Betty could do was to pull the skin together with adhesive tape. Then Betty gave her additional medicine and bandages. The people who brought her insisted on our taking a live rooster as a gift, so we tied it on top of one of our loads, which were at that point being carried down to the water's edge.

During our stay in Yajiang we had often watched the process of craft crossing the Nya or Fish River, either skin coracles or the larger wooden ferry. Slightly to the north of the town stood the piers for a bridge which had been built by a German engineer, then destroyed during border warfare. Some people said that the boatmen had ruined the bridge so that their trade would be restored. The ferry was attached to ropes on each shore and was propelled by poles as well as by the swift current. Oarsmen also sought to guide the craft. This day a detachment of Chinese soldiers, fresh reinforcements for the Litang garrison, got to cross first. Our group made the second trip, complete with all our bedrolls and saddlebags. Each trip the ferrymen pushed the ferry upstream and close along the shore before suddenly pushing out into midstream. Here they started to row frantically as the current whirled the boat around. Their efforts then took the ferry out of the midstream rapids. When we made the trip, it was surprisingly brief excitement with spray dashing over us, and then we were coasting toward shore on the other side. We released our grips on handholds and hastened to scramble down a plank and off. Next we watched the loading of horses on the ferry, their hooves clattering madly as they reared and plunged with fear. One of them did jump off the ferry as it approached the side where we were waiting. It was swept down a little way, but then it emerged dripping wet on the bank.

We were interrupted when Betty was asked to come up the hillside to a village where someone was sick. She turned out to have several patients. One was a boy with a large growth on his abdomen, and she recommended to his parents that they take him down to the Catholic hospital in Kangding since she could not help him.

By this time the loads and yak had also been brought across the river. Someone told us our new riding animals were ready for us outside the house where Betty was caring for the needs of the sick. She hurried to finish and then put her medicines back in a saddlebag. As we came out, we watched an officer mount a very stubborn mule. A split second later he was sailing through the air over the mule's tall ears. What broke the suspense was when we all saw that instead of landing on one of many boulders, the man had eased his fall by landing in a five-foot pile of manure!

Just after the upset, Betty found her own animal very restive as she mounted. The men standing around her tried to reassure her that it was not serious, just sores on the poor animal's back! Fortunately, once she was seated astride the horse, it started out in a placid way. The caravan was leaving, and Phillip called out, "Come! Come! We need to keep up with the soldiers. The forests ahead are dangerous because of bandits!"

Before the next day of travel, however, I had applied ointment to the sores on the horse's back as well as adjusting the pads and saddle blankets with Phillip's help. The horse seemed to be relatively comfortable when Betty's weight was on it. That was good considering the fact that our journey stretched for eight and a half hours, most of it traversing the three summits of the Rama La.

Jamba's horse got so weary crossing these mountains that by afternoon it finally just lay down and refused to carry him any farther. He had to walk the rest of the way, leading his horse. Around us were soldiers straggling along. Some of them were so tired that they would grab hold of the tail of a horse in hopes that it would pull them forward.

Poor fellows, these forty men did not look much like soldiers. Most of them had only straw sandals on their feet and rough Tibetan wool cloth wrapped around their legs. Some were assigned to carry cooking utensils, large iron cauldrons and pots. Others had bamboo carrying poles over their shoulders to handle food stuffs in wooden buckets. Of course, they preferred their usual rice to the barley flour so commonly eaten by the Tibetans. We, however, relished the roasted and ground barley, finding it very convenient and nourishing, especially on a cold winter's morning when we had no time for cooking.

On this stretch of the trail we began to use the large tent we had brought along because we were getting into more desolate country, above cultivation and the homes of farmers. Beyond the forests we entered the high grasslands, home of the wandering black tent nomads. Jamba, Phillip, and I could get the tent up quite quickly if the wind wasn't bearing down on us. Also I discovered how hard it was to get tent pegs out of the frozen ground in the darkness of early mornings. At that time the tent would also be stiff with frost, so we had to jump on it to fold it into a decent size roll. That part of breaking camp was sort of a game we men played, and it warmed us up a bit.

The days were crisp and clear, and our eyes would search the horizon. Sometimes a nomad encampment or a "mani" pile of stones would break the monotony. Tibetans carve the words of the mantra, "Om Mani Padme Hum", on flat slabs and place them face out on a rock pile. Over the years the pile would grow longer and longer. Occasionally we saw a tall "chorten", a monument holding the remains of some venerated saint. A mani pile nearby would invariably vouch for that deep respect. Our companions would circle these, chanting prayers and sometimes throwing another stone on as an act of worship. We were now far above the tree line. "It won't be much longer," Phillip told us, "and these stretches will be really empty, even of nomads. They have to move their flocks and herds to lower elevations in deep winter."

The high altitudes affected our breathing, particularly at night. We would prop our heads up on saddlebags to combat the feeling of suffocation we had when lying down flat. In two weeks we had traveled about 100 miles westward toward Batang, approximately half the way. On arrival in Litang Phillip took us to the local clinic where a Dr. Hsiao, the dispenser, lived. Hsiao, being from Batang and a member of the church there, gave us a warm welcome. "I know of an unoccupied house up the street where you two can stay," he said, addressing us. "We can fit Phillip and Jamba in here, but that will give you a quieter place."

We had barely moved to our quarters when we heard a knock at the door. It was two Chinese soldiers delivering the gift of half a load of wheat to us from the Colonel Fu we had met in Chengdu. Along with the gift was an invitation for us to attend a feast at his residence. We were surprised to learn that the Colonel was in Litang rather than Batang, but our immediate question was what gift to send back to him with these men.

"How about the brand new wool shirt I have in my saddlebag?" I suggested to Betty.

"Would that be enough?" she replied. Eventually we decided to add a large tin of hard chocolate for someone of his standing. If we had been able to get into our loads, it might have been easier to find something suitable.

At the feast Colonel Fu told us, "I have stayed here in Litang because of some disturbances among the tribes which I have to settle." The local Washi were on the warpath with the Sangchen to the South. "But I'll help you get transport," he promised. "And I insist that you let me loan you two rifles and ammunition for your own personal safety as you go on to Batang. You can turn them in to the commandant there on arrival."

I thanked him for his thoughtfulness although I didn't intend to use a rifle myself. It was a long time since I had been on a rifle range, and I hadn't set any records as a marksman. I was sure that Phillip and Jamba would be thrilled to be able to carry them, strapped to their backs! I just hoped that we wouldn't have another accidental shot fired at the wrong time or place.

Betty and I looked up at the massive Litang monastery as we walked away from the military buildings. It housed a famous printing establishment, using carved wooden whole page blocks to produce the Buddhist Scriptures. Below it lay the crowded old town, a cluster of homes. We skirted this as we walked down into the broad strip of the new town with a row of connected one story buildings on either side. It held a scattered number of people, a few horses, and several dogs. Come dusk any grazing goats or pigs would be brought back and driven into the front door of the owner's house and through to a small back yard. Then the doors would be shut and bolted for the night. Up and down the street other doors were shutting, too.

One night while there at 14,000 ft. altitude Betty began to get a gaspy feeling, and at the same time she couldn't get the zipper of her sleeping bag undone. "Help me out of this!" she begged. I hastened to help her, and once free she said, "That took all the self-control I could muster not to go to pieces while you worked on that zipper!" I knew what she meant, having been trapped the same way myself. To add altitude breathlessness to that was a bigger test. "Brave girl, and lots of spunk," I thought to myself. "But at least we are half way."

CHAPTER 6

MAKING FRIENDS OF THE UNFRIENDLY

D uring our ten day layover in Litang we were guests of the Hsiaos, having our meals with the family and their occasional visitors. While Hsiao had not attended medical school, he was called a "Doctor" by both Tibetans and Chinese. And we gave him the courtesy title as well. His practice had given him wide experience because with no one else closer than at Kangding to refer patients, in emergencies he was sometimes forced to improvise. "Oh, yes, among my patients I've had some whose hands had been amputated for stealing," he told us. "Lots of gunshot wounds, of course. I do the best I can with God's help."

Then the time came when some Washi nomads offered to take us to Batang. These were of the same tribe which had so recently been fighting with the scrappy Sangchen nomads to the South. We asked if our fellow travelers from the last caravan would be going along as well, and the answer was, "Our animals are tired, and you are the only ones we will take on this trip." No further explanations were offered, and we gladly accepted the chance to go on.

By now we were in December and eager to get on our way before the winter deepened. Even the postmen were sometimes stopped then by the snow. The Hsiaos helped us provision, and at last we rode off. Below Litang we passed the farmhouse where one of the former Dalai Lamas was born. Then our caravan started out on the vast plain where in summer ten thousand animals could be seen grazing, less at this season of the year.

Betty noticed one young driver who was limping badly. Feeling sorry for him, Betty asked Phillip, "Will you try and find out what's wrong? Perhaps we can help him."

He came back with a surprising report: "He got his sore leg from a beating by one of Colonel Fu's soldiers. The colonel called in the nomads and demanded that they take you to Batang. When this fellow objected, that's when he got hit with a rifle butt."

"Oh, that's awful!" Betty said. "I guess these men must blame us a bit for that."

"No, I don't think so," Phillip said. "Anyway, they'll soon get to know us. When I told him you could give him medicine for his sore leg, he said, 'Good'. That's a start."

The first day on the march is almost always a short one. Thus it was early afternoon when Betty gave me some Balm of Bengue to take over to the lame driver. I went to where he sat with some of his companions. I was a stranger, but I wanted to be a friend. The ointment was my peace offering, and he accepted it. With that we began to feel a sense of belonging. I thought of some fifty years that missionaries had been going through this region, seeking to enter into the life of this people, so perhaps we were benefiting from the established reputation of earlier pioneers.

At our campfire that night our talk with our companions strayed to the way the Dalai Lamas are chosen. The farmstead near Litang, called a "yapshi" in honor of the seventh Dalai Lama being born there, was in our minds. After a Dalai

Lama dies, a search is made for a successor. A child candidate is discovered when he meets several physical specifications as well as being able to identify some objects used by the Dalai Lama. These searches have produced new Dalai Lamas from as far away as Mongolia, a country which practices Tibetan Buddhism. Now I asked, "If Dalai Lamas have come from Chinese-controlled sections of Tibet, like Kham and Amdo, doesn't that show that Tibet is actually much larger than the maps drawn by the Chinese government?"

Phillip and Jamba thought this was a great joke. Finally Jamba spoke up, saying, "Tibetans don't pay attention to lines drawn on pieces of paper by outsiders. We are one people wherever we live in our country."

We then turned to discuss the route the caravan was taking. "There are several trails we could follow," Bema explained, "but these nomads want to go a bit northwest in order to pass close to their home encampments." It was at the end of the next day that our caravan was attacked unsuccessfully by robbers as described in Chapter 1, though our caravan leader may have hoped for a somewhat safer passage through this very lonely territory.

We were now in such open, barren country that even in following one route a caravan could shift considerably from left to right as long as it finally arrived at an appropriate river crossing or a campsite. A route was defined by viable passes, and sometimes there were more than one option when it came to those. We certainly never saw a signpost or bridge, so the nomads must have had their own markers or instinctive sense of direction.

The farther along we went and the closer they got to home the more cheerful they became. They didn't seem to mind the cold and must have chuckled when we dismounted at times and walked stiffly to get some circulation and warmth back in our feet.

Fording streams that were partly frozen required a

75

certain knack we didn't possess, so we let our horses choose their own footing. I recall a time when Betty's horse started in ahead of mine. It skated on a piece of ice and then broke through and into the water. Up on the ice again and then another crackling sound and two hoofs in the water. The climax came when it faced a high bank on the far side. This proved much too slippery, and the horse reared back on its hind legs and fell. While I gasped, Betty kicked free of her stirrups and smoothly slid off its back. Without her weight the horse regained its balance and clambered up the bank, then waited for her. Some of the rest of us clustered around, but she cheerfully shrugged and said, "Not a bruise! I think that I'm learning what to do in an emergency."

The seventh of December I greeted Betty enthusiastically with a "Happy Birthday!", but we were soon riding once more on what would be nine bitter hours. The night before the wind had been so fierce that we had had to pitch the tent below a ridge and on a slanting piece of ground. Now we headed up and over the fearsome Hari La, weaving our way among great boulders. At times we were close enough to the loaded yak to observe them sometimes squeezing through narrow gaps. Of course, their loads would take a beating, but that is why they were covered with dried yak skins.

The last stretch up toward the pass the wind struck us with terrific force. Even with scarves or handkerchiefs to cover our faces, we travelers had to turn our heads to one side to avoid the full force of the gale. The snow felt like ice, as the wind dashed these rough particles at us. I even had them inside my goggles. The animals were covered at the front with hoar frost from their breathing. The poor creatures hung their heads down and kept grimly on.

If I had something I wanted to say to Betty, what I yelled was blown away. Either that or the wind blew the sound back down my throat! Since Jitsen, the caravan leader, had passed the word along that we could be in danger of bandits on this pass, we noted many spots up ahead which looked like excellent places for such an ambush. We took comfort in two men sent ahead as scouts to check if the trail up to the pass was safe. When they returned with the word that it was all clear, the caravan got under way again. On the other side we continued to contend with ice under the snow, and we were a weary lot that stopped at some sheep corrals in mid-afternoon. The stone walls gave us welcome windbreaks, and soon people were relaxing and having some warming tea.

I fished out our camera. "Here, Betty," I said, "Let's get a picture of you on your birthday. This is special, your first one out in the Tibetan wilderness. And I took a picture of her, all bundled up and leaning against a low, stone wall.

"We've got to celebrate," I added and held up three different tins of C-rations. "You have your choice, and it will be a change from our regular fare." So that night we divided a GI tin we had bought in Chengdu and savored its wieners and beans.

Later the nomads were also in high spirits. When one of them named Aden came over for some medical help, his friends crowded around, laughing and pointing at the white bandage Betty was tying on his grubby arm. It was indeed a contrast to his butter-smeared skin. Tibetan nomads don't go in for frequent baths, for they like the protection grease can be from the cold.

Another night we were camped in a grassy valley at a lower altitude. Here we were surrounded by thick forest and behind that towering snow peaks. Long after we turned in, the full moon came out and bathed the valley in silvery light. The nomads were still seated around their campfires when they must have noticed that a slight chunk had disappeared from the moon above. They know just what they are expected to do on such an occasion – get together and build up their fire, then chant against what they believe is some evil power trying to devour the moon. As we listened, their prayers mounted, louder and louder.

We watched this scene from the door of our tent. A dark shadow was covering more and more of the face of the moon. To us it was obvious that it was an eclipse of the moon and that the shadow was the shadow of the earth. To them it was a titanic battle in the heavens.

They were getting hoarse by the time the darkened moon finally had a fresh, new sliver of light appear, then more and more. I imagined Tibetans all over Tibet looking up into that night sky in those moments when they savored their victory. They had their moon back! Superstition, yes. Myth-making, yes. But this seeming struggle was in its own way a means of coping with the mysteries in life which they did not understand.

Of course, those cries of victory around the nomads' campfire may have cloaked some fear and an immense sense of relief that the demon wolf had once more been foiled in his attempt to swallow the moon. According to them he had to disgorge the moon and allow it to shine once again. And they felt that they had had a share in this triumph of good over evil.

Afterward the moonlit valley lay quietly before us. A grave danger in the skies had been averted? But hadn't we been warned that wooded areas like this were prone to harbor bandits? Nothing dangerous like that happened that night, but a month later we heard that three men were robbed of everything they possessed at that very campsite.

Moving on, we came to the village of Samba, a scattered number of farmhouses with no central cluster. Even as the Rama La had been the site where a foreign child had died, so Samba had the grave of a traveling missionary, William Soutter. And here in desolate, wintry Samba, our nomads offloaded us, promising us it would only be for two days, and drove their yak off home. It was rather eerie to be so suddenly divested of the caravan, left with our loads in a stranger's courtyard in the middle of nowhere. As long as

Phillip and Jamba assured us we could count on the nomads' return, why should we worry? There was so much we were unfamiliar with we might as well find a cozy spot and rest. I suppose that the long hand of Colonel Fu had something to do with our young men's supreme confidence in the nomads fulfilling their commitment to take us to Batang.

We had barely settled our bags when a Tibetan couple in sheepskins presented themselves, asking the "doctor", meaning Betty, to come and see their little son. He was a toddler who had fallen into a kitchen fire and been badly burned. As she went with Phillip, he mentioned to her that this sort of injury was very common and usually fatal. When Betty saw that the child had wet cow-dung slapped over his burned arms and hands, she quickly got to work, washing these off. Little Tsering was amazingly brave and uncomplaining though he winced as she had to separate his fingers, which were stuck together. She bandaged each finger separately, using sulfa ointment.

The stopover at Samba was marked by the special joy of meeting that one child's desperate need. By the second day he was already showing some signs of improvement. That night the nomads had returned as promised with fresh animals. They were obviously keenly interested when they saw little Tsering and his bandages. Betty told his parents, "If he doesn't heal up, then bring him over the Draga La to Batang, and the woman "doctor" there will give him more medicine." Fortunately this wasn't necessary, for Tsering did heal up completely. "Thank God for the medicine," Betty said, "but the Lord's power is at work as well."

The last pass, the Draga La, was between 17,500 and 18,000 feet high. The day we crossed it much of the snow had melted, but the ascent was extremely steep. Our horses would take a few steps and then have to stop, breathing agonizingly slow. We crisscrossed up the side of the rock-strewn mountain, right and then left. Betty was glad to hang on to the pummel of her western saddle. Looking upward, we saw what looked like an impenetrable wall; only to find at last the cleft which would let us through. Passing by huge, towering cliffs, we came out on the other side and commenced a precipitous descent. Down, down, and more down, so rapidly that we almost wished for a bit of climbing again. Then abruptly we reached a clearing with a house or two and stopped. This was a small place called Barjuki, the end of the line for the yak because the Batang valley below it was too hot for them to survive in.

The nomads pulled loose the straps and lifted our loads away from the yak. We gave them the balance of their pay, and immediately they turned and started driving their animals a bit higher for good grazing. The men were not noticeably demonstrative. It was not their way, but we knew that we parted good friends.

Phillip bargained for donkeys from among those kept at this place, sufficient to handle our boxes and other goods. We still had our horses for the trip down to the valley. Before long we were met by some Tibetans from the Batang mission, and they told us that Miss Schwake was waiting for us at the gates of Batang. Phillip began recounting to these friends some of our adventures on the road. Then we caught sight of the sheltered valley, its townhouses, farmhouses, and in sight on the road a foreign woman, her grey hair pulled back in a tight bun. She was surrounded by a cluster of Tibetan women and children. We had reached Gladys.

"You made it!" she declared with satisfaction, hugging Betty and giving me a warm handshake. Stepping back, she looked at our faces which were burned by the sun and peeling. "I know how I look – a fright," Betty laughed, and we all laughed. Gladys then introduced us to her Tibetan friends. That accomplished, she said, "Come this way. It's not far to our Jaboding." The streets were paved with cobblestones and wide slabs. On either side the walls of

Tibetan houses rose, pierced by a few doorways. Curious faces peered out at us. Then we took a turn to the left and out into the open. Descending to a stream full of watermills, we crossed a wooden bridge. Then we climbed on the other side to the gate of the mission compound. The grounds inside had two livable buildings left from what had at one time been quite a community. The area was mostly a large fruit orchard, standing leafless this time of year.

"There are nine acres of land in Jaboding," Gladys told us, "and the missionaries built a water channel which turned it from wasteland into this garden. These buildings were erected between 1908 and 1910. I stay in what used to be the doctor's residence, and you will be in the old hospital building, up on the third floor." She stopped, panting for a moment, and then continued to talk.

"Oh, it's going to be so good to have you here. And Betty, you're going to be such a blessing right away to me. You see, I can't pull my own tooth, and I have a molar that has been giving me a lot of pain. I want you to take it out, the sooner the better."

Betty was nonplussed but tried not to show it. She had pulled some teeth in the past but never a molar. She had visions of wrestling with a tooth she couldn't extract or, even worse, one that might break off. And then what would she do? Gladys, supremely happy, seemed prepared to leave it all to Betty.

"I don't have a lot of experience," Betty hedged, but Gladys would have none of that.

"A lot better to trust you than to make a trip all the way to Kangding or Chengdu for one tooth," she chuckled. "I'd have to leave you in charge of the clinic here," she said, "and you wouldn't want that, would you?" And her glance was decidedly impish.

"No, I wouldn't. Not that fast, but I'll see what I can do with your molar," Betty replied.

CHAPTER 7

ADAPTING TO A MAKE-DO SOCIETY

B etty had laid out her dental forceps and other slight store of equipment in preparation for removal of Gladys' ailing molar. Beside this she had her dental course notebook, ready for emergency reference. "Whatever are we going to do for a chair that will tip back?" She asked me.

I experimented for a while and finally came up with a straight chair tilted back against a crate, a board then tied to the back of the chair in order to provide an extension. I added a pillow. "I'll have to hold this chair steady," I told Betty, "but it's the best I can do as long as Gladys doesn't want to wait."

Then we sent for Gladys, and Betty got the offending tooth out without any injection or anesthesia. Betty was delighted that it came out intact because she had had visions of what it might be like if it broke, leaving the roots behind. "Here's an aspirin," she said to Gladys. "I don't know which of us is most relieved, you or me!"

We soon learned that Gladys was accustomed to accepting less than first class treatment. The joys of being "beyond the ranges" compensated for a lot of inconveniences. For example, Gladys had been without glasses for a year. That meant she depended on her faithful helper, Guei-yin, or Phillip to read the small print on medicine bottles in the clinic. She still played the wheezy organ in the chapel without trying to follow the printed music. "Plenty of people in Batang have poor eyesight," she laughed. "Nobody here thinks I'm peculiar, and like my bad tooth, I just couldn't leave and go off for weeks to get new glasses."

As we settled gladly into the first apartment which we had for ourselves after two years of married life, we had to make-do or go without. Gladys saw that we had a wood stove and a small cupboard in our kitchen. At first we sat on boxes and trunks in the living room area. Then for the bedroom Gladys was able to provide us with two doors laid on saw horses. Betty sewed up a huge cloth bag into which we stuffed straw, and this was our mattress. It was notably uneven after we lay on it for a while, but definitely an improvement over our canvas cots. Once we had curtains up, we felt quite civilized. But in our bedroom we hadn't paid attention to a flue opening in the ceiling. One night we were awakened by a loud thump, and once we had the flashlight on, we saw a rat sitting dazed in the middle of the bedding between us. Horrors! But not for long, as he hopped off the bed and scuttled away! Though I chased after him, it was too late. Coming back, I finally realized where he had come from and knew that I'd have to block that hole as soon as possible.

Within two weeks of our arrival Christmas came due, but when I asked Gladys about how the Christians of Batang would celebrate, she said, "Our festivities will be rather quiet except for carol singing." Then she brightened up and said, "Let's see what we can do. I've been so busy with the clinic and the orphans that I haven't given it much thought. Have you got any ideas?"

"How about a Christmas tree?" I suggested.

"I've often wished we could have one," Gladys replied. "Getting a good fir tree is easy enough; my problem has always been that we don't have any Christmas ornaments to put on it. All I have ever been able to locate in the store-rooms is a box of clip-on candle holders. And since we don't have any little candles to put in them, they have been no use to us. In the absence of missionaries here some years ago as well as the warfare that has gone on right in the middle of the compound, the place has been picked over and cleaned out of nearly everything that used to be here."

By this time a little wonder in my mind had blossomed into a big wonder. "Could you look for those candle holders?" I said, "I remember that we brought along some packages of small candles from India. Maybe they would fit your candle holders."

Sure enough, they fit firmly into the holders, ancient numbers such as I had never seen before. They probably had been brought across the Pacific by earlier missionaries, up the Yangtze River, across Tibetan trails. Now we could use them once again "for such a time as this", holding these lights and reminding us of Jesus, the Light of the world.

On Christmas Eve the Christian community crowded into our living room where a tree stood tall to the ceiling. It was covered with about forty candles, which we had carefully placed with the constant thought of fire hazard. Then Phillip and some of his friends lit the candles as we began singing, "Silent Night". I had tried to imagine what a candlelit tree would look like, and I was transfixed by the simple beauty of what we had before us for a brief time. We didn't have any of the traditional decorations, but nothing else was needed.

Christmas morning I said to Betty, "You know there are no stores, and I haven't been able to get you anything. We can probably find something out of our boxes to give

Gladys." And Betty replied, "Well, I haven't been able to get a present for you either. Last year in Darjeeling I knit you your scarf. Somehow this year with all we've been doing, it escaped my mind. I guess this Christmas we'll just have to say that we are ourselves gifts to one another."

"Yes," I replied, "and we've also got living here in Tibetan country to be thankful for."

"How about helping me with Christmas dinner, so that we'll be ready for Gladys?" she said. It was no everyday menu which we served up. We had canned turkey which we had purchased in Chengdu. Gladys had supplied apples from the Jaboding orchard, so that turned into an apple pie. With cheese! We also began with soup, followed by creamed fish on toasted brown corn meal muffins, and served the turkey with mashed potatoes, squash and gravy. That was a luscious memory later in the winter when meat was practically unavailable.

We foreigners were not living in isolation, of course. Far from it! As Betty and I looked down from the interior porch to the courtyard below, we could see cows, donkeys, chickens, and a horse. The donkeys were by far the noisiest. But we also had the occasional chatter of the families housed with us in this large hospital building. As I was passing a doorway there one day, a man named Hosang asked me if I would sell him the sewing machine we had brought with us. He knew it was a brand new hand operated model, but the handle for the grasp had broken off on the trip into Batang. Betty was dismayed because we had no way of repairing the cast iron. "I don't think I'll be able to use this," she had told me. Somehow that information had traveled mouth to mouth, reaching him.

Before too long Hosang was the proud possessor of our sewing machine, and we were the possessors of a small milk cow along with a number of Tibetan silver rupees. The next thing we knew he had acquired a treadle frame and placed the sewing machine on top of it, linked up with a sturdy leather band. With this in shape he started to work on the balcony outside his family's rooms and developed a thriving business. The sunshine kept him warm. The machine hummed in spurts. He was happy, and so were all the rest of us happy for him.

We had a storeroom off the courtyard where we stabled our cow. We had to take care that neither she nor the donkeys got into our supply of turnips down there. In the absence of stores with bins of vegetables, everybody had to listen for news that someone else was selling grain or potatoes, salt or sugar. Then it was first come first served until the supply on sale was exhausted. Since we were in language study, we arranged for the able help of a young woman named Lozongdrema in our kitchen. She was far more proficient at searching out food stocks than cooking to our taste. But that latter would change. The first day she arrived, her face was deliberately blackened like a chimney sweep, a Tibetan custom with some to indicate modesty. Betty insisted on compound standards of cleanliness, hot water and soap. Only then did we see her rosy cheeks, so common in this cold climate. Nevertheless, Betty noted that she sometimes came with bruises which Betty gradually elicited were the result of beatings her mother gave her when drunk. The mother, whose name was Gye-nga or Fifteen, seemed placid enough when she came daily to milk our cow. Her Buddhism, however, didn't give her real peace in her life.

Farmers in the valley were planting their winter wheat in January. We had a period of three months when our potato bin was empty, so when Gladys suggested that we get a local farmer to work a garden plot for us in Jaboding, we were very receptive. Dendru, the man we got, started to work, following our instructions, but suddenly we found that he had gone ahead on his own and planted all our small store of precious onions. They were all we had at the time to flavor our bland diet of turnips. Betty demanded of Dendru that he dig up all the onions and return them to the store-room. This he did with very poor grace. He continued to sulk until one day when he fled to our place for refuge. He sat on the floor in a corner of the kitchen and refused to tell us what his problem was. At last he divulged that he had a quarrel with his wife. Then in his rage he had stabbed her. Now his concern was what her relatives might want to do to him in retaliation. We certainly didn't sympathize with what he had done, but we served as go-betweens in settling the incident. From that time on Dendru seemed to regard us as his benefactors. Again we were getting below the surface of Tibetan culture and forming relationships.

Happy-go-lucky Phillip with whom we had traveled to Batang had come from a very poor Buddhist family. He could not forget his childhood when other children laughed at him and his brothers for picking dandelions, nettles, and pig-weed greens for food at home. When his older brother died of typhoid, his father took the body and threw it in the Batang River. The water was low, and the body snagged on something. There it stuck, bobbing up and down. Little Phillip (or Yama Drolma then) went down to the river bank twelve days in a row until finally the body swept away. Moving from that type of trauma into the release of faith in a powerful and caring Savior had transformed him while he was in middle school.

One day a group of young monks from one of the local monasteries brought one of their number to Jaboding, seeking help. Gladys was away at the time, and Betty took the case. The young monk had some deep cuts in his scalp, covered with cobwebs to staunch the bleeding.

"How did this happen?" she asked, as she began to clear away the cobwebs.

"He did it to himself," was the surprising answer. "He

took a meat cleaver and hit himself on top of his head several times."

Betty could hardly believe her ears. "He did it himself? Whatever for?" she asked.

"His lama teacher wouldn't give him pocket money when he requested it. He came back to the dormitory so angry that he decided to end his life."

"Oh, that is the way it happened," she murmured thoughtfully. She had been dabbing gently at the wounds, but she decided to bear down a bit even if the antiseptic stung. Her patient was not clean shaven, and with his hair beginning to grow out it was hard to clean the mess. He groaned, but she gave him little sympathy. "He wasn't in any great danger," she told me afterwards, "and I figured it might do him some good in the future to suffer a little pain for his stupidity." Again we were gaining insights into Tibetan life situations.

Teacher Atring was another character from whom we learned a lot beside Tibetan language. A little, bent over man, conspicuous for his enormous, floppy, felt hat, he told us incidents in the history of Batang. "My father was the chief steward of the prince of Batang," he said. "The princely house is no more. Early in this century the Chinese general, Chao Erh-feng, arrived here and captured the city. He was furious because of the large number of his soldiers we had killed. Such a cruel man! My father was among those he slaughtered. Yes, my father was paraded out and beheaded. I rejoiced when that Chao was himself executed by the Chinese government for his misdeeds."

"Then you must have known Dr. Shelton, too?"

"Yes, I was here when he was shot by bandits and carried into this very hospital to die. Have you seen his grave?"

"I have been over to the Christian cemetery," I replied. "There I saw his grave and also that of the young doctor, Dr. Loftis."

"What a pity the young one died such a short time after he reached Batang. Two or three weeks it was. He caught smallpox from a patient."

Atring's weathered face told me of many sorrows. He had known the French priests, two of whom had been killed. One of them had had his skull made into a drinking bowl. Atring had witnessed the destruction of the mission school in the battle of Jaboding. There we sat in our living room in the hospital building with the wind whistling through its old bullet holes. It was history writ large!

A hen's clucking two floors below had Betty's attention. "Excuse me," she said, "One of our hens has laid an egg, and I must get it before someone else claims it as from her hen." Soon she was back with an egg in her hand which she then took to the kitchen. When she returned, we resumed the lesson. Teacher Atring understood how precious each egg was to us. For my part I was admiring at how Betty could distinguish the sound of our two hens from others in the courtyard, and I could remember how she had once said to me, "I feel as proud of our hens as though I had laid the eggs myself. We're getting an egg nearly every day!"

CHAPTER 8

SIZING UP POWER STRUCTURES

Tibetan New Year holidays were a major Buddhist festival time, graced by crisp, sunshiny weather in Batang. Teacher Atring volunteered to take Betty and me to visit the monastery, saying, "The monks want you to take pictures." He had seen some which Betty had taken and developed, including one of himself. He probably had hatched the idea, but we were pleased anyway to be able to observe the ceremonies as sort of media representatives!

The monastery was a collection of closely connected buildings on the west side of town. As we approached its walls, we were caught up in a flow of people going to see the masked dancers perform. Passing through a main gate, we came out into a large courtyard, already crowded. The people were being shoved back form the center area by husky guards – monks with fearsome black grease circles around their eyes and black marks curling up from the corners of their mouths. They bore long staves and were prepared to use them on unruly monks or laymen.

The monks who danced portrayed the forces of evil with

their hideous masks, but the forces of good which came out to vanquish them wouldn't have won a beauty contest either. The papier-mâché masks were blue, green or black, depicting deer, pigs, and demons. Other dancers were dressed as skeletons, and they whirled around in circles. Most players wore gorgeous silks and swayed ponderously about. Some of the singers repeated their routine over and over between acts, accompanied by a cacophony of trumpets, flutes, and drums. These performances were brand new to us, but even Tibetans who saw them every year had not tired of them. Old plays were all the better for being familiar, and adults could explain the meaning of what was going on to their children. We took pictures from time to time but finally wearied of the slow and repetitious action being staged.

Teacher Atring was not surprised at our short attention span and took us next to a lama's apartment. It was cozy and clean inside. The monk ushered us to seats on a rug-covered platform and served us butter tea and Tibetan cookies. We picked up these stringy pastries and found them quite tasty. When I asked the monk how often he visited his home, he said, "Three or four times a year, but, of course, this is really my home now."

After that we strolled through the monastery, seeing the prayer hall and the kitchen with its large tea vats. In a chapel filled with images we came up to a small crowd around a brightly dressed monk. "What's this?" I whispered to my teacher. He replied, "This man is the oracle of the monastery. Most days he wears red robes like the other monks, but today you see him wearing the oracle's robes. When he puts them on, another spirit possesses him, and he can answer people's questions."

"Don't all lamas answer questions for people?" I asked.

"Yes, they do. Questions about when to start a trip, whether to buy a field, who to marry. But this oracle is much more powerful. He takes the difficult questions, and he gets very well paid!" This he said with a cynical grin.

The crowd around the oracle was growing, and he was beginning to shudder. We could barely see what was going on, so we moved on out of the jammed room. "So you think the oracle can read the future?" I asked Atring.

"Why, yes, he has made some good predictions," he replied. "Why do you ask?"

"Well, Buddhism does not really teach divination. Seeking to know the future is more a worldly desire. It does not provide any merit. Why then is this practiced in a monastery?"

Atring looked at me sharply, and then said, "But this is our Tibetan custom. We have always done this."

Buddhism had its origin in India where it has largely died out. The teachings of its founder, Gautama Buddha, spread to various parts of south Asia, up into Tibet, and also to China, Korea, and Japan. In the process this religion adapted and changed some of its teachings and practices to fit different cultures. Tibetan "mo" or divination is probably pre-Buddhist, but it is still a very valued practice.

Buddhism does not teach the existence of a God who is either Creator or personal. Thus it has been called atheistic. And yet its teachers are called gods, the three aspects of godhood being the Buddha, the Doctrine, and the Priesthood. Questions of logic and consistency didn't bother Atring. "Buddha gave us 31 commandments," he confidently told us. "The other religions of the world were founded by six apostates from Buddhism."

The next big event at the monastery was the installation of a new abbot, a child in the countryside selected as the reincarnation of the former head lama. The abbot had died several years before. Following classic custom, the lamas searched for a child born at the approximate time of the old abbot's death. Several candidates had been found and tested as to their recognition of various possessions of the former abbot. When this child passed this examination and reached the age of seven, he was ready to enter the monastery to be trained for his future career as the new abbot. He was escorted from his country home to Batang.

Even the Chinese officials were waiting to honor the boy abbot. They had deputed some of their troops to lead his procession into town. The horses of the monastery were decked with ribbons of blue, yellow, and red silk. Their bridles were works of art – brass, silver, enamel, and tooled leather. And the saddle rugs were equally resplendent. The mounted priests escorting the little boy were wearing mulberry-colored brocade, glistening with gold and silver threads, and odd-shaped hats. The boy did not ride. He was seated in an elaborate sedan chair and was dressed in bright red and yellow silks. After the Chinese authorities greeted him, they fell in line beside his chair. The cavalcade moved slowly through town and on to the monastery. When the child arrived and was helped to descend from his chair, he could hardly walk because his Tibetan boots were too big and still stiff. Some of the head monks assisted him on both sides and, thus supported, he went in to his throne room.

A genial monk then ushered us into a guest room prepared for a series of feasts. Rows of low seats, carpeted with rugs, lined the sides of the room. In front of these seats were tables loaded with cookies, apples, and tangerines. The feasts would continue for seven days in order to include everybody of any consequence in Batang or from outlying regions. And the guests, of course, brought gifts with them for the boy abbot.

*Later on, welcoming a Buddhist abbot from
Dawu at our home in Ganzi.*

In the course of our eight months stay in Batang we
witnessed three such displays of ceremonial pageantry. The
third was the celebration which occurred when the abbot of
the Litang monastery arrived in Batang on his way home
from the capital city of Lhasa. The old post road from the
West passed right beside the mission compound, so we had
a spectacular view of his caravan. First to arrive were the
pack animals, part of a total of 300, the lead mules decked
in red ruffs and with bells jangling from their necks. Those
load animals carrying personal baggage of the Tibetan

prelate were ablaze with yellow silk spread over the loads, and each one had a flag sticking up from the pack saddle with his name embroidered on it. The servants who escorted these animals were dressed in yellow silk blouses and maroon robes. They hailed us, and we waved back. It was a dramatic event in which we were glad to play a bit part.

The local Batang nobility had ridden out to meet this special caravan. Now they came in all their finery, followed by some Lhasan nobility. Some of their hats were a sight to see – deep crowns of yellow satin covered with designs in gold and silver, fur ear flaps flaring out every which way. Most rode stately black mules whose paces were marked with superb footwork.

The leading lamas of the local monastery had also traveled out ten miles to welcome their distinguished guests and were mounted and dressed up for the occasion. They wore hats of great variety: towering hats, peaked hats, and platter-shaped hats, each kind indicating a different rank in the hierarchy. They were accompanied by monks on foot, playing flutes and blowing trumpets in a riot of noise.

Then the outstanding part of the parade came by – a stately mule carrying a bundle of silken clothes which was covered with a piece of yellow silk. These garments had been worn by the Dalai Lama, and he had presented them to the Litang Monastery as a treasure. These would make a display there for worshippers to venerate.

Accompanying this great gift was the Litang abbot, a big man riding a beautiful light tan mule. He merited a golden hat and a long quilted cloak of yellow silk, its ends tucked under him. The unexpected modern touch was that his eminence wore glasses. Behind him a man rode, holding a yellow silk umbrella with long tassels. This couldn't possibly shade the high lama but was a due mark of his distinction.

As I watched, I thought of how many great processions

had traveled this road. In the early part of the century the ambassador from Nepal had come this way en route to the imperial court in Beijing, bringing what the Chinese called tribute, what the Nepalese called gifts. His largesse extended to the missionary doctor then in Batang, for the ambassador presented him with an elephant tusk.

The Tibetans are masters of gaudy drama, and this has roots in feudal pomp. Such actors require an audience of common people, whose drab lives are brightened by this symbolism. Crowds lined the road and eventually gathered in the monastery courtyards. Because Betty had a camera we were able to climb up to rooftops in the monastery to enable her to take pictures of the crowd scenes. It is noteworthy that though maps would show Batang as part of a Chinese province that we saw it when it was a completely Tibetan town.

We even were allowed into the private quarters of the young abbot. This was unusual because generally women were forbidden in the monastery buildings, and not even female animals were supposed to enter the precincts.

Teacher Atring had once told us, "Tibetans always reverence animals, particularly marmots. Do you know why? No, of course, not. Marmots stand up out of their holes on the plains and they look like they are praying. So we say they are incarnations of the monks." He also informed us that Tibetan wedding customs call for the groom and his party to hammer on the gates of the bride's home at midnight for entrance. When they have been let in, the gates are shut again, and within the house the feasting begins. With our own acquaintance with the Bible this custom had a familiar ring.

Of course, the term "midnight" should not be taken with any precision. Exact time meant little or nothing in Batang. We rarely used our own timepieces and learned to judge time by the sun.

It was the custom, when we were invited to a feast, for the host to send a servant to call us to the feast many hours in advance. The servant would make a second call in mid-afternoon. By the time he put in his third appearance we knew it was time to walk over to our host's house.

Gladys told us, "If you want to return hospitality, prepare a foreign meal. The people here in Batang are very interested in what foreign food is like. I've found that the most acceptable gift I can give at any time is cookies. These became so popular that I was besieged with requests from various ladies for me to bake cookies for them to use at their feasts. I finally had them come over here and gave them lessons on baking cookies for themselves."

With Gladys as instructor, Betty learned how to make rough candles from yak fat poured into intestines, using a thin stick wrapped in twisted cotton for a wick. Betty tied the bottom of the intestine around the stick, and jammed the end of the stick into a turnip or potato to hold it up. When we lit this type of candle, the smell of the casing as it burned was terrible, and we kept scissors handy to trim the edges. Thus, when Wangden, who lived in the other third floor apartment, told us he was going to try and extract fuel oil from fat pine, we were excited at the prospect of having the use of gas pressure lamps for a change. The equipment for this extraction process had been lying around in a storeroom. Wangden was successful, and we all gathered round when he pumped up the first beautiful, bright light. Soon several of us had lamps functioning. The light shining from our windows couldn't help but be noticed in town. Soon Wangden had requests from officials for the precious fuel, one of them being Colonel Fu, who had reached Batang. Wangden couldn't refuse such powerful people, so what started out as a simple experiment turned out to be a frequent job for him. It also generated a lot of appreciation around town.

Men in Batang didn't usually work too hard. A third of a

day's work was quite standard unless it was harvest time. Workmen expected to be paid three times the usual wage to put in a full day's work. Of course, the altitude of around 9,000 feet may have had something to do with this easy-going pace.

Hoshang, the tailor in our courtyard, was expanding his work force so he could make shoes. His helpers talked or sang at their work. One man would process wet hides by hand and foot to produce usable leather. The cloth uppers were dyed bright colors and set out to dry. This schedule was quite capable of interruptions, however, such as for a picnic excursion to a nearby hot spring.

From our balcony we could see another resident bring home his catch of fish, while they were still alive and flipping. He would put them in the little water ditch outside the front gate until such time as he could sell them to some of the Chinese in town. For the men it was often quite an amiable and leisured existence. The same could not be said for the women. It was they who hauled heavy bags of grain to the mill or water from the stream, and at other times they might well be carrying a child on their back.

Betty and I applied ourselves to the onerous task of sorting out the differences in an eastern Tibetan dialect as compared to the Lhasa Tibetan we had studied in India and found in the literature. In Batang the consonants are softer. Many of the terms are different. Nor are this or other dialects close to the stilted language of the religious books. And we found especially difficult the honorific terminology used when addressing a superior. The ordinary name for "horse" was "ta" while the honorific term was "chippa". The subtleties of tone and idiom required both hard study and use of the language daily.

When we read the literary language to a Tibetan, we needed to rephrase it with, "That is to say, in Ba-ge (the speech of Batang)," And added to this mental and verbal effort, we were trying to understand Tibetan perspectives, such as one of Atring's remarks, "Tibetans see no point in worshipping a good god. Why bother to worship him if he won't hurt you anyway?"

The time came when Betty and I were ready to deliver our first talks in Tibetan in the chapel meetings downstairs in the hospital building in which we lived. Betty's first talk was on the verse, "Where your treasure is there will your heart be also." The very next evening as we were again gathered in the chapel a fire broke out in one of the apartments. Someone at a distance noticed the smoke and came running to warn us all. The fire was quickly extinguished, but Betty and I, remembering all too well the train fire in which we lost our outfit in India, realized that we had almost had to the opportunity to go through a second such loss!

Through the spring Batang was abuzz with reports of violent internecine fighting among top religious leaders in Lhasa. During this period when the young Dalai Lama had not assumed his full powers, a former regent and the current regent had gradually become antagonists even though they were high lamas, the head of Sera Monastery and the Dalai Lama's teacher. This led to plots, ambush, a package bomb holding a grenade, a suicide, and the imprisonment and the mysterious death of the ex-regent, Reting. Civil war was narrowly averted, and the average Tibetan prayed earnestly that the Dalai Lama would yet be protected in order to assume his office. "It hardly sounds like Shangri-la," I commented to Betty. "It certainly reminds me of the fighting our teacher in Ghoom, Tupchen, went through in

Lhasa years ago."

At this point we also received disturbing reports from "down country" as we called Chengdu – where Chinese currency was losing its value, the Communists were becoming ever more threatening, and the Nationalist government was struggling. We were glad that we had moved as swiftly as we had to position ourselves out in Batang. We were not far from a small pass called the Bum La where in 1727 the country to the West was handed over to the Dalai Lama under the suzeraininty of the Manchu Emperor while to the Tibetan Princes in Batang, Derge, and eastward were given the official seals recognizing their feudal control of eastern Tibet. Of course, those old agreements had not been honored of late. Colonel Fu himself had at one time been Mayor of Batang and resident in the former princely palace there. This prince had been beheaded, as was Teacher Atring's father, back in 1905. Their crime was rebellion against Chinese authority. Small wonder then that the Khambas continued to be restive and even at the time we were there occasionally besieged Chinese garrisons.

CHAPTER 9

THE POWER OF EXAMPLE

❈

With the coming of spring to Batang we discovered to our surprise that the fruit trees originally brought in by the missionaries had spread over the entire valley. Every direction we looked we could see the blossoms of apple, peach, pear, and apricot. The fruit would begin to be picked in the summer soon after the June barley harvest.

Once the fruit began to ripen in the Jaboding orchards, every available person was drafted to watch the laden trees by night. Five tents were pitched at various points. The watchdogs on the compound were on duty as well. By this time Betty and I had a large white dog which Gladys had given us. We named him Dongwa, or White Bear, and he was a beauty as well as one of these watchdogs.

Gladys was very generous with the fruit crop, presenting much of it to friends, selling the rest both as fresh fruit and dried. Since the drying operation took place on the second floor roofs, right outside our windows, we could see the sliced fruit spread out in the sun. And when thoroughly dried it was handy and delicious to munch on.

One day we all had a close brush with danger when a mob from town chased a mad dog up our hillside and through the main gate into Jaboding. The poor creature was being stoned as it ran, so it ducked into our courtyard. There it met and aroused Dongwa, and they circled growling at one another. The stranger dog clambered up the steps to the second floor balcony, followed by our dog. He then ran over and down the other stairs and out of the court.

Parents in our building had been dragging their children inside doors. The pursuers down below were shouting to them, "Mad dog! Mad dog!" Then the dog dashed out and on across the fields. Before too long a stone found its mark, and the chase was over.

What everybody realized all too well was that a bite from this crazed animal could spell a terrible death for any such victim. Gladys had no serum for rabies, and we were too far away from any hospital to get some in time. Though we had heard Gladys' warnings about being alert regarding dog bites of any kind, I had already had one dog sink his teeth into one of my leather boots. Another time a dog had slashed my hand. Now here was a verifiable sick dog at close quarters. I wondered later why someone hadn't shot it to death, but I expect stones were closer to hand as well as people very expert with throwing them. Also, bullets were expensive as well as not so available.

I went down to check on Dongwa and found he had bloody foam on his white ruff. We then examined him more carefully and couldn't detect any scratch on his skin. I cleaned him up, and then we decided to tie him up for a few days of quarantine. Poor pup! He certainly was dejected, and we had no way of telling him why he was being punished. At the same time Gladys' gardener was nipped on the hand by a pig and then ran a fever. She kept a close eye on him, but he made a quick recovery. Dongwa was finally released, and the hysteria died down.

In the midst of Gladys' clinic work and the supervision of the entire compound activities, she sometimes felt the need for a little time to herself. Her special place to retreat was a seat under an old tree with a flower bed of geraniums near by. Everyone understood that when Gladys went there, she was not to be disturbed.

At other times she relaxed by talking with us. "We were on the trail once," she yarned, "and we came to a dangerous bend around a huge rock. It looked like an impossibility to squeeze around the narrow ledge with our riding animals. But we prayed, and we made it. Then later I learned that we had other help that day. My mother and a close friend of hers back in the States both woke up at midnight when it was noon for us at the rock. They felt a special burden for our safety, and they prayed for us, too. I've still got the letter she wrote with that welcome report."

"Gladys," Betty said thoughtfully, "How long is it since you had a vacation? You know what I mean – just dropping every responsibility and getting away for a few days of complete relaxation."

"I've dreamed of that," Gladys replied, "but there are always people I need to care for. Little Nadanee, for instance." She was speaking of a fragile three year old boy with a broken femur, dislocated hip joint, and a hunchback, whom she had taken in.

"Surely you have enough helpers so that you could get away for a few days," Betty continued. "If you went away somewhere in the valley, you would still be within call if there was a dire emergency." But Gladys was not to be persuaded.

Later when we were by ourselves I said to Betty, "The only way you'll ever get Gladys to have a break is for you to insist and then offer to go along with her." And when Betty approached her that way, Gladys showed interest in the proposition for the first time. She even admitted that some Tibetan friends near the north end of the valley had often urged her to come out to their homestead for a rest.

Some days later they were off for a week's stay in the guest room of Gladys' friends. I walked along with the two of them to help carry their supplies. We skirted the town, crossed the river on a wooden cantilever bridge, and then walked northward to their destination.

Back at the compound in addition to my three hours of Tibetan in the morning, I started some extra classes in Chinese in the afternoon with Wangden, who was an evangelist. He was not only handy making lamp fuel but had graduated from a Chinese Bible school. Betty walked in to town once to pick up a few more supplies. The butter out where the two ladies were staying was standard Tibetan butter, somewhat on the smelly side and holding strands of yak hair. Betty had learned from Gladys how to boil and strain the butter we bought. This is one item she wanted to get. "If my mother got hold of raw Tibetan butter," she said, "she would hold her nose with one hand while throwing it into the garbage can with the other."

"Take some fruitcake back with you as well," I said. "In the mail two late Christmas packages have come. One of them was mailed a year and a half ago to India, and at last it has reached us here."

Since there was still some snow on the passes, I was a bit embarrassed to think of a postman gamely carrying the weight of those packages on his back to us.

When the two ladies returned from their vacation, Gladys had a bunch of letters which she had written. I was able to give her higher denomination postage for the envelopes because the local postal station only had small denomination stamps. Due to inflation one would have had to cover the envelopes with those stamps. Fortunately I had gotten a good stock of higher denomination stamps while in Kangding, so I was able to supply her with these more suitable stamps.

"The battle of supplies" we used to call it, and we soon

realized that Gladys with a large number of people depen-
dent on her faced far more severe testings in this area than
we did. For example, we had discovered that telegraphic
transfer of money from Kangding to Batang cost a 25%
surcharge. Getting money transferred through banks from
Shanghai to Kangding cost 40% of the amount transmitted.
Thus, the only practical way to get hold of a remittance was
to discover a merchant or a private individual who wanted
funds down country and would make an exchange with you.
Occasionally a local person might want funds in India or
some other country and could provide its equivalent in local
silver or goods.

Gladys and Betty came back much refreshed, and a
good thing that was, too. Awaiting them was a stream of
patients. Betty had a portly lama with a severe toothache. I
tilted a chair back with books under its front legs and
supported it from behind with a bench up on its end. The top
of the bench was the head rest. She went right to work, and
with her strong wrist she extracted the offending tooth. Talk
about gratitude! The priest was thrilled to have it out and
gave her three Tibetan rupees.

One night we were called from supper to a home where
two women had been fighting. The stronger of the two had
been stomping on the weaker, who was four months pregnant. The two were still shouting at one another, and the
room was filled with other people talking at the top of their
voices. The mother of the woman on the floor was drunk
and shouting. Betty gave her a determined push, and she
went over to the other side of the room to continue yelling.
Eventually we restored a measure of calm as the malcon-
tents drifted off into other parts of the smoky house.

The greatest display of industry that we saw in Batang
came in the month of June when harvesting erupted in fields
everywhere, followed by winnowing. It was a great time for
singing as work crews in different places chimed in around

the valley. When the crops had been gathered, the grain was beaten out with flails on the flat roof tops. There the workers were even more visible to us, close enough for us to spot five or six groups at a time. They were in such good spirits and sang so well that they lifted everyone else's morale. Betty commented, "They're just as hard-working as the harvest crews on my uncle's farm in Ontario, but what a difference a combine would make if they had one!"

Like farmers elsewhere they wanted to get the precious crops in lest a storm damage them. In fact, later we did get rain and flooding. The small stream between us and the town became a raging torrent, and we were cut off. Then as we watched we saw one of the watermills break up and collapse into the water, millstones and all. We felt sorry for the owner and his family as they fought fruitlessly to save their precious mill.

That summer our plans in reference to the length of time we would stay in Batang moved into high gear when Betty and I realized she was expecting our first child. Gladys was not at all eager to be responsible for the delivery the following winter, and she highly recommended to us the French Catholic lady doctor back in Kangding. Almost at the same time she received word that her fellow worker, Melba Palmer, had reached China from furlough in the States and that a young family, the Backs, was also preparing to join them in Batang. Moreover, we also had news that our own recruits were coming to Kangding. We felt free to leave Gladys and marveled at how well everything was fitting together for all three of us.

We knew that Betty needed to get under way without delay and take advantage of the milder summer weather. When we began to look for a caravan, we found one in the process of formation. This one was primarily for two Tibetan ladies, one the matriarch of a wealthy family and the other the wife, a third one, of the local Chinese military commander.

This young woman was well along in pregnancy but was being sent to her husband's home for the birth of her child. "We are very glad to have you travel with us," the elderly Madame Ghey told Betty. "Then if Madame Liu has any medical problems on the way, you will be there to help her."

"We are very glad to have you travel with us."

Betty commented to me afterward, "That could be the infirm helping the infirm! In spite of that, I like the look of Ghey tai-tai. When she spoke to me, she had a mischievous grin on her face. I think that she is genuinely going to be a pleasant companion on our trip."

By early August we were packed and ready to leave, our loads well covered with yak skin, provisions carefully calculated, and a light tent pieced together from tarpaulin and some blanket material we had bought in India. The tall canvas tent we had used on the way out to Batang? It was more suited to winter use, and we had loaned it to Gesang, the air force pilot who had visited his parents in Batang. He completed his visit home soon after our arrival and welcomed the use of that tent for his winter trip to Kangding. However, his caravan was attacked and robbed en route of most everything, including our tent. To our surprise later a prompt government counter attack resulted in the recovery of some of the booty, including the tent. So eventually it had been delivered to our co-worker, Edie Seager, in Kangding.

These days Lozongdrema, our kitchen helper, seemed so moody that Betty finally asked her, "Why are you so sad? Is it because we are leaving?"

"Well, yes, I wanted to learn more about cooking and baking," she answered, "but now my mother is arranging a marriage for me to an old man. I don't want to marry him, but what can I do?"

We were quite horrified at that prospect, and the upshot was that we offered Je-nga a more lucrative deal than the marriage would have offered – employment for Lozongdrema with us in Kangding and sizeable remittances from her salary to be sent back to her mother. The mother agreed. Though Lozongdrema said little, she must have been ecstatic in her quiet way, and she did allow herself a smile or two.

Being with Gladys had been a delightful experience for us, a person we would never forget. Perhaps she is best summed up by something Phillip told about her. He said, "When I went off to boarding school in Kangding, as a new student I had a miserable time. The older students would say of us entry level boys, 'Your footprints have no long standing here.' Then one day I received a package in the mail. This was unheard of. Then I opened it and found that Aunty Gladys had sent me some lovely cookies! I can't describe how happy I was." His gratitude to her was a factor in his accepting Christ the next time he revisited Batang. We also were thankful for the fun times we shared with this outgoing missionary nurse.

Dongwa, our dog, would be traveling with us, a treasured gift from her. For days I had been taking him on long walks in order to firm up his foot pads for the rough surfaces he would face on the trail. Many Tibetans had tried to buy him from us, but he was not for sale. Mischievous as ever, one morning just before we left he got into the kitchen and drank up the morning's milk, where it sat in a pan on a low stool. What a rascal! I let out a shout, and he made a rapid exit. He certainly considered himself a member of our family. Rascal or not, we couldn't leave him behind.

CHAPTER 10

TABLES IN THE WILDERNESS

V arious members of our 26 member party left at different times to reach the yak caravan in the mountains.
Our friends walked with us as far as the hot springs where
we farewelled. As we mounted and headed for Barjuki, the
side valley was already in shadow, and we felt the chill. I
pulled a sweater from behind my saddle and slipped it on.
The road was familiar to us, and we felt like old hands.
After so much preparation and so long a wait, we were
thrilled to start off for Kangding.

We met the nomad drivers with their yak at Barjuki. Up
we started to the first pass. It was clear of snow, and the view
from the top spectacular. Now the grasslands caught our
attention with the beauty of their summer flowers. We went
on to the Haji La and crossed it this time easily. When we
reached a campground, I made a deal with a member of the
party to give us part time help. This Tsering scoured around
for brushwood to burn. Lozongdrema used some of this to
build our fire, and then sensibly suggested that we put the rest
of the firewood inside the tent. It fit handily under our cots.

The next morning we found the camp snowed in, and we were the only ones with dry wood! Everybody else had left their wood out. Thus, after our fire got going, we had one man after another come over with a metal dish to beg some coals from us. We were glad to oblige them and make this contribution to the breakfast fires of all the rest.

The nomads had killed a yak, and then tied big slabs of raw meat on top of some loads. When birds tried to peck at the meat, the drivers would scare them off. But they would use their own knives to slash off some raw meat for themselves to chew on. We travelers were also able to buy some of the meat and try our best to cook it, no mean feat at high altitudes.

Two nights before we rode into Litang we camped not far from where we had been attacked on the trip out to Batang. And we were attacked again, this time late at night. It started with the dogs in the caravan barking, White Bear joining them vociferously. The marauders fired at us. But once they heard the strength of the return fire, they lost interest in pursuing their attack. The shouting and noise in our camp went on for a long time after that, and none of us got very much sleep.

One morning White Bear stayed where he had been lying under a cot, even after everything had been dismantled. We had to help him get up, and he could hardly walk. His paws were tender and his muscles sore. If this got worse, we had the option of slinging him up on one of the load animals, but it never came to that. He limbered up and was never so helpless again.

Ghey ma-ma, the matriarch, and young Mrs. Liu wore wide-brim straw hats to shield themselves from the sun. Betty had a sun hat like theirs and wore it occasionally. But if the wind came up, it was a doubtful blessing. Mrs. Liu was well along in her pregnancy. As a result we were all sort of holding our breath should her horse stumble and fall, taking her with it. To avoid this possibility, she always had someone lead her horse, holding the bridle. One day she actually had some slight contractions. Betty got busy and gave her medications which cleared this up, and everyone was much relieved, not the least Betty.

Our stop in Litang gave Betty a bit of a rest from that responsibility. We three stayed with Dr. Hsiao and his family, whom Lozongdrema knew well from when they had lived in Batang. What a view we had of thousands of grazing animals on the plain before us, so many more than the previous November when herds had been taken to lower pastures! The grassy flowers were out in profusion. "We Tibetans call our land 'medo-yul' (flower country)" Lozongdrema told us. "This is the first year I have been able to see how it is in the high country for myself."

Tsering left the caravan in Litang, and we didn't try to replace him. We found traveling in summer so much easier and with Lozongdrema along that we could manage by ourselves. Coming up to a nomad encampment of ten black tents one day, our party got permission to stay overnight with them. The hand-woven tent we were in was 40 feet long and could easily accommodate the family and us, assorted ewes and lambs, and the goats which crowded in near edges. Everybody in the tent slept with feet to the fire, a circular row of rolled up bundles like the spokes of a wheel. Overhead we glimpsed some stars through the smoke vent. These nomads seemed inured to the cold, the men often baring their shoulders, dropping their sheepskin robes to their waists while we snuggled into all we could wear. Their children, so rosy-cheeked, stood around barefoot, surreptitiously looking at the strangers.

One day the three of us lagged behind the rest of the party with the load animals. Then the yak drivers decided to stop to brew some afternoon tea. They herded their animals together to graze in a field while they got a fire going with a goatskin bellows. Betty, Lozongdrema, and I decided to go on rather than wait for the men to have tea. Instead of the open country we had expected, we reached a heavily wooded area where we were passed by two heavily armed Tibetans. They rode on, and we began a slow descent through the trees. It was eerie, for the pine needles deadened all sound. Suddenly we felt very much alone and began to speak in whispers. We knew that this was the most likely place for robbers, and we were unarmed. It was too late to do anything about our stupidity in venturing off by ourselves except pray.

All of a sudden we were startled by the sound of a gargantuan laugh from up the hillside, a tremendous bellow that went on and on, pealing through the forest. It was most extraordinary, and we looked at one another in puzzlement. Had those two men we had seen circled around and followed after us? Or was a woodcutter observing us from a distance and finding our plight amusing? Whoever he might be, we had the feeling he could see us, and we certainly couldn't see him. We urged our horses on and soon broke out into a clearing and then the open road again. At last we could laugh at ourselves and vow not to go off on our own any time in the future.

When we reached the Rama Pass with its long section at the top, it was clear of most snow. We recalled how we had plodded through the drifts the previous November. After we settled in at a campsite below the pass, we noticed two horsemen approaching on the trail. Ignoring the others, they came right over to our campfire. They dismounted, and one of them, a young, man, came toward us with a broad smile on his face. He knew who we were, but we couldn't place him. "You're the doctor," he said to Betty, "and you fixed the sore on my leg last year when you passed through Yajiang. You gave me medicine to put on it. I did everything you said. I changed the bandage as you told me to do. And look at my leg now!" With that he pulled his sheepskin robe aside and proudly pointed. Where formerly he had had a large, running sore, now nothing remained but a faint scar.

This former patient, Dawa, had heard the news that we were coming along the road, and he had ridden many miles from his homestead to find us and to thank Betty. He went back to his horse and unslung his gift, the carcass of a goat, and came over to lay it at Betty's feet. "Thank you," he said, "You are a good doctor! If you would come and live in my country, we would welcome you."

"We have not yet decided where we will live," she replied, "Will you not sit and rest after your long journey?"

"We must return soon in order to get home before dark," Dawa replied.

"But at least you two will have time for a cup of tea," she answered. They readily agreed and sat cross-legged by the fire to drink from the cups Lozongdrema brought them. Betty reached into her pocket and brought out some dried apricot slices for these farmers to snack on. They liked them so much that we gave them some dried apples to take home. "This fruit is from Batang," we said. "There are so many fruit tress there."

"Oh, yes," Dawa replied, "We have all heard about the fruit of Batang, but this is the first time I have tasted it." They mounted and rode off. "That was good of them to come so far just to say thanks," Betty said, and I agreed. How responsive Tibetans can be! And how amazingly informed about what caravans are passing through their territory. Not a jungle telegraph perhaps, but certainly a network of word-of-mouth communication. For the first time we realized that this seemingly empty country could well be abuzz with word of our passage through it.

And now what should we do with the goat? We three certainly couldn't eat much of it. "We'll share it with the whole party," Betty said. Soon the goat meat was boiling in a pot, and Madame Ghey got the ladies together to roll flour dumplings. We were at a high altitude, so the meat would be tough and the dumplings heavy. Still it was a feast, and everybody had their fill. "Have more! Have more!" Madame Ghey urged us, but we felt that we had consumed a respectable amount. The caravan men saw to it that the pans were scrapped clean, and even the dogs had the bones and scraps.

Madame Ghey got the ladies together to roll flour dumplings.

In a day or so we dipped down into the cleft through which the Fish River flowed and crossed by barge to the town of Yajiang (or Nyachuko in Tibetan – Fish River Crossing) Betty again had a stream of patients at the door of our room, for she had an established reputation in this place.

"People keep asking for the green pills," Betty said to me. "Remember that man who came to me the last time we were here. He pressed his stomach as though in great pain, and I gave him some green soda bicarb tablets. And he came back the next day to tell me how much better his wife was feeling! Those pills are priceless for pregnant women with heartburn. No wonder they are so popular! I keep getting asked for green pills!"

From Yajiang our caravan was made up of "ula" transport, the animals forced from local farmers as taxation and provided to official travelers at reduced rates. But this meant that we changed animals more frequently. The two ladies we traveled with had the proper papers demanding a supply of animals for our whole party. Headmen sometimes were slow to meet the demand for horses and yak from the various homesteads in their district. If homes were scattered, it could take a day or more to assemble a new group of animals. A farmer would send somebody from his household along with his animals. Madame Ghey had approached Betty in Yakiang, saying, "We find ourselves short of money for our 'ula'. Would you have any extra which you could loan us until we can pay you back in Kangding?" We lent her some money, figuring we had enough left over for our own needs at our next stop to change animals. That was at Dungolo where we found the headman upset at the arrival of our caravan. "I've just supplied animals for a caravan heading up the other road to Ganzi," he declared, "It will take us some time to locate some more for your caravan." Madame Ghey urged him to find riding animals so that we could at least go ahead to our next stop for the night, leaving some servants to wait for yak to take the loads on. The headman agreed to do this, and we began to pay for the "ula". To our surprise he had upped the price beyond the amount that we had set aside. What would we do out there in the middle of the grasslands? Had we made a mistake loaning money to Madame Ghey in Yakiang? We didn't think so, and then happily this very lady came over to us. "Here," she said, this is the balance of your money which we didn't use. Thank you again for your help." What she gave back to us took care of our lack, and we went on our way rejoicing. Two more nights on the road and no more changes of animals, and we would be back in Kangding! Madame Ghey had instructed two of her servants, "Whatever happens, see to it that at least you bring our food loads for our use tonight."

That afternoon when we stopped at a farmhouse, we recognized it as the same one we had stayed in when we first crossed Jeddo Pass. Lozongdrema had us assigned to the same third floor chapel we had slept in before. Betty edged up the notched poles with care. We always carried some food in our saddlebags, so soon we had some refreshment. Then we waited and watched, hoping to see some sign of the load animals coming. The sun lowered, and the shadows lengthened, and we still saw nothing moving up the valley from Dungolo. Just at dusk, someone downstairs with good eyes spotted something on the trail. Whatever it was, it wasn't much. When it got closer we saw it was a man leading a donkey, carrying two loads. At last we could identify it as our bedding and food supplies. We were rather embarrassed to be the only ones to get our baggage and offered to share food with the others. "No, no, thanks," said Madame Ghey, "The people here have already assured us that they would provide us with food, and it will be very warm down here by the stoves tonight." We never did learn if her servants got a scolding for their failure to bring her necessities, but all seemed smoothed over in the morning.

We were all saddled and ready to go, but it was quite late in the morning before the load animals finally appeared. Our party didn't wait any longer but spurred their animals and headed toward Jeddo Pass. It was a beautiful day as well as a fairly short stage. After cresting the pass, we descended to the Jeddo community, that wide scattering of miserable huts. We stopped at one of the dingy inns and settled in. Later the yak caravan shuffled in. The next morning we rode ahead again, the last few hours to Kangding being over a better than average road. The two of us were some contrast to the way we had left the previous fall. Instead of hanging on with all available hands and feet, breathing all kinds of unuttered prayers that nothing would happen to disturb our horses' frame of mind, we were now bent on hurrying them up, trotting quite a bit, and merrily using a small switch to produce the desired results. After all, we had crossed 12 passes over 15,000 feet during the past days. This stretch of road was a piece of cake. We rounded a spur and saw the tile roofs of the city. How modern it appeared and so completely different from nomad tents and fortress homesteads! We dismounted as we reached Kangding, and walked down the busy streets. White Bear kept close to us at this point but looked very confident. At a turn in the narrow streets we said our farewells to the Batang ladies and went on to the corner house on the square we would now call home. When we arrived, Edie introduced us to Margaret Miller, who had shared the house with her in our absence. Then they showed us how they had fixed it up. "I have rented a place across the street," Margaret told us. "I'll soon have some members of my own mission coming, and I'll be ready for them."

"Put your things in the front bedroom," Edie said. It was only 9:30 in the morning, and the sun was streaming in the windows. We had made it, twelve mountain passes, rugged country, and now back to our border base. The house would have enough space for our reinforcements with some crowding. Meanwhile, breakfast was served, a feast — eggs and bacon, toast and jam!

"What are your plans?" Margaret asked us.

"Well, obviously we'll stay here for a while," I said "and that means Tibetan language study. We had an ex-lama, Kesang, traveling with us. He said he would consider teaching us. We'll see whether that develops."

Summer travel had been much easier than the wind and ice we faced the last winter. However, on our 23 day trip back to Kangding we had some rain every day as well as high water in the streams and rivers. This meant that our first job on arrival was to open every load to look for water damage. Even with yak skin covers the boxes and trunks were not necessarily water proof. We hung many things out to dry and had some mould and rust marks, the ordinary wear and tear. What mattered was that Betty had arrived safely.

CHAPTER 11

GOD'S BREAKTHROUGH COMES

❧

O ur preoccupation with Tibetan language and people as well as where our group should work was rudely disturbed by further news of Communist advances down-country. There the Nationalist government had just dropped any pretense of making peace with the Communists, once again naming them outlaws and calling for their suppression. But how? In two short years the Nationalist forces under arms had lost 50% of their numerical lead over the Communist armies, the proportions dropping from four-to-one to two-to-one. The increasing flow of American aid to the Nationalists, both militarily and under the UNRRA relief organization, did not check this steady attrition. The government in Nanjing was alarmed, and so were the people under their control. That included Chinese in Kangding. Suddenly old-time residents were recalling how the Communists, on the "Long March" in 1935-36 had their Fourth Route Army pass near this area. Down at Luding their troops clambered across the swinging bridge on the chains, the wooden planks having been removed, and captured the Nationalist garrison. Kangding, easy to defend because of the limited access to the city was spared. Yet the Communists had roamed at will in other parts of eastern Tibet, living off the land and people and camping in Batang, Litang, and Ganzi. Mao Zedong said of this trek, which he himself experienced, "This is our only foreign debt, and some day we Communists must pay the Manze (savages, an epithet used by the Chinese regarding the Tibetans and tribes people) for the provisions we were obliged to take from them." In view of Chinese governments' repeated claims to own Tibet, this reference of Mao's to "foreign debt" must have been a slip of the tongue on his part.

While a Nationalist General Chang saved Kangding when the Communists approached in the 1930's, a General Ma had failed three years before that in dealing with danger within the city from his own discontented troops. They at that time mutinied and killed him because they had not been paid. A local businessman, who had often suffered levies to pay the soldiers, said to me, "If the soldiers are paid, we have no trouble, but if they are not paid they become bandits." Now in 1947, fear was rising again because with the paper currency constantly being devalued, the rank and file military were becoming dangerously restless again about their pay.

Under these circumstances we were not surprised when the local government occasionally made a public show of force. One day we heard a commotion outside. Glancing out our living room windows, we saw that a mass of people had gathered in the square below. We heard a roll of drums, and a procession emerged from the law court up the street. It was a detachment of armed guards, and there in their midst we made out a Tibetan, his arms tied behind him. A condemned prisoner no doubt, for he had a board sticking up behind his head and shoved down inside his collar. This board bore a sign in Chinese characters declaring his alleged crime.

Our cook, Ahnu, had joined us in order to have a good view, and she calmly told us, "He is on his way to execution." We were shocked to witness this dazed man being hauled past our windows. "Where are they taking him?" Edith asked. "He will be shot to death outside the north gate." she replied. The crowd closed in behind the drummers, and the square soon emptied of people. Obviously they didn't want to miss the spectacle. This event was regarded as a treat and a warning, and we understood some spectators would go on from the execution grounds to the nearby baths at the hot springs to discuss it afterwards.

Saddened, we asked Ahnu if she knew the circumstances for which the Tibetan had been condemned. She looked grim as she replied, "He's not guilty. He is suffering because the government wants to punish someone, guilty or not."

"But what is he supposed to have done?" I asked.

"A postal runner was robbed of his mail, and when he tried to hold on to it, he was badly wounded. The government was very angry that mail was seized, and they were determined to find a culprit to punish. They took this man, tortured him for a confession, and condemned him to death even though he had a good alibi. My friends tell me that he had nothing to do with the robbery."

Thus, day by day, we would be drawn to our windows, usually because the normal hum had been punctuated by shouts or other outcries. It might be a mother beating her child or one of the Chinese merchants having a dispute with a Tibetan customer. Then we witnessed a woman being tied to a lamp post while the police were being called. This was an elderly Chinese accused of stealing from a shop. We were amazed again at Ahnu's seeming grasp of the affair. "She's well known," she declared, "because she comes from a wealthy family. But she has become an opium smoker and has used up all her money. Now she steals in order to buy opium." The police led the little woman away, her head bowed low, and the crowd that had gathered dispersed. But the next morning Edie happened to look down into the street below and noticed someone slumped on the ground four or five feet from our front door. She called us all to look. While we watched, a well-dressed Chinese gentleman walked up, stooped down, and dropped some black pellets in the hand of the person lying motionless there. We guessed that the man had probably brought the poor unfortunate person some opium.

We turned again to Ahnu for information and she said, "That's the woman who was caught yesterday," she said. "The police beat her badly and released her this morning. She has no one to care for her. Think of it. She used to own a store of her own!" That set us buzzing about what if anything we should do. A blanket perhaps? A cup of water? Should we carry her inside? We wanted to rush out and be good Samaritans, but we also knew that this could lead to serious complications and law suits. Somehow, reaching out to give aid in a case like this was somewhat complicated for us newcomers.

While we were still debating what to do, a Chinese nun came along, stopping briefly by the woman. She took command of the situation. Since the chapel steps nearby were where unemployed carriers waited for work, she found a porter. They came back, and the nun helped load the woman on his back. Edie exclaimed, "She's taking her to the Catholic hospital! Let's at least give the nun some money toward hospital expenses." And this we did.

The next day we heard that she had died. Discussing this with the French nurses on one of their visits to check on Betty, they told us that they had eased her last hours. "She was too far gone. We have many desperate cases like that," they said. "So often it is too late to save the patients. The most helpless are the tea carriers who come up here. If a tea carrier gets sick, the innkeeper will simply carry him outside and leave him to die in the cold." I remembered then seeing a tea carrier lying on a mat outside an inn and wondering what he was doing there. Now I knew. And perhaps all of us would be better prepared as to how to respond next time we saw such a desperate need.

These hospital sisters were obviously experienced but not made callous by the hard cases they faced. We admired their high spirits. "We find we have just one serious problem," Sister Miriam, the head nurse, laughed, "So often when we sit on beds in homes around the city we pick up lice. We always have to inspect our robes carefully when we go back to the convent after these visits. Our problem until recently has been that we had no electricity, and it was hard for us to see the lice so we could get rid of them."

"You don't have electricity?" we marveled, "In this city where the water power gives us such good lights?"

"We are Franciscans," was the reply, "and thus we own nothing. We are dedicated to simple living, but we talked it over. We decided a little electricity might save us from typhus. So then we made our request to Bishop Valentine, but he turned us down. He told us that it was a frivolous request for Franciscans to make. Of course, he and the other priests have electricity! We prayed then that he would change his mind, and God answered our prayers. One day electricians installed the wiring, but we are only permitted 15 watt bulbs. That's still an improvement that we appreciate."

This fall of 1947 with the arrival of two more workers for us, Margaret Landahl and Hester Withey, we at last were more of a team. Margaret seemed in some ways more Chinese than American in her outlook, born and raised in China, a veteran missionary and fluent in Chinese. Hester found everything vastly different from the Africa which she had known as a child and youth. She had graduated from university in Cape Town. As an R. N. she had brought along a good supply of medical equipment and medicine along with her expertise.

On their bus trip between Chungqing and Chengdu, Hester had her first opportunity to use some of her medical supplies! The dilapidated vehicle had rolled to a stop, and one of its wheels was smoking. The driver was desperate for some grease, and Hester inventively produced a tube of Balm of Bengue. With that on the wheel the bus was soon chuffing down the road again.

Hester, Edie, and Betty were all prepared for clinic work of our own in the near future, and thus they had a lot of questions to ask the nuns who staffed the hospital. Of course, Betty was frequently seeing the doctor and the head nurse for prenatal care. The shy French doctor and her tall, commanding assistant, Sister Miriam, were always welcomed to have tea when they made a home visit at our house. Our ladies got well enough acquainted to discuss with them questions of the Christian faith. At first terminology was a problem, but once they sorted that out, they all found themselves on common ground on essentials of faith rather than works as well as the "amazing grace" that our Lord supplies us. This kind of friendly dialogue was unusual in mission circles in the 1940s, for Protestants and Catholics tended to mind their own business, go their own way, and have little contact with one another.

Shortly before the expected birth of our first child, our neighbors, George and Pearl Kraft, warmly invited Betty and me to be their house guests because their large mission home would be warmer for Betty than the wooden structure in which we lived. Then George nobly accompanied me up the deserted streets to the Catholic Hospital at 2 a.m. one night to call the doctor for Betty. At the gates, we called for three quarters of an hour before the hospital gateman stirred, and he was unwilling to open for us. George finally said, "Call one of the sisters to come down here," and soon a sister spoke to us through a crack in the gate, assuring us that the doctor would soon come. And she did, and all went well.

A day or so later, Betty was still in bed but with a high fever. The baby was in a crib on the other side of the room when a strong earthquake struck. By the time George and I sprinted up the stairs to the room, the tremors were over, but we all noticed a large crack in the ceiling right over the crib! And a chunk of plaster had fallen in the place where the crib had been formerly! A few years later this 75-year-old building was to be so badly damaged in another earthquake that it had to be demolished. This earlier deliverance filled us with gratitude for God's protection to Betty and our little daughter, Marion Elizabeth. Rare penicillin soon brought Betty's temperature back to normal. The doctor's bill for the delivery and a total of twelve visits was eight dollars, which we insisted on doubling at the very least. The sisters' attitude then was simply, "Our time is God's!" And our hearts echoed, "Yes, our time is God's, and our times are in his hands."

Before long we moved back to our front bedroom in the corner house on the square. Baby Marion slept in a bureau drawer instead of a crib for lack of space. From the windows of this room we had a front row seat on an opium den right across the street. Opium was both raised and freely sold in this area, the trade being the private preserve of the local Chinese governor. The then central government way down in Nanjing knew about this but could not stop it. Opium was a problem to the Chinese, but fortunately the Tibetans shunned it. We recall a prostitute thrown out of this brothel, standing in the street below us and moaning. How close we were to human tragedy! If it wasn't this, it could be across the square where a Tibetan boy, fighting another Tibetan, picked up a stone and pounded the other's head with it. One day I saw a man, carrying a lot of prepared food, stumble and spill the lot. While a crowd gathered, he picked up what he could – meat balls, potatoes, lentils – and a beggar scraped up what was left on the street before the dogs got their chance at the scraps.

That winter Paul Lindell and Fred Renich, who had been among the original recruits for Tibet, paid us a visit. For their first breakfast with us Betty served them butter tea and "tsamba" or barley flour, giving them the necessary instructions how they should proceed. They made a valiant attempt to eat in Tibetan style but weren't making very good progress. When Betty thought her joke had gone far enough, she signaled Lozongdrema, who then brought in the foreign style breakfast that was ready and waiting. Paul and Fred gladly pushed their tea bowls back and wiped their hands. "I'll go for the eggs and toast," Paul said, "I think we can practice on the tsamba another day. By the way, I had some long talks with a high lama on the road here. I was speaking in Chinese, for I found what I learned as a child coming back to me. And somewhere he had studied Chinese, too. He had just attended the National Assembly as a Tibetan representative. One night I turned an orange around an oil lamp to explain to him how the earth has night and day. The next evening as we rested from the day's trip, he asked me if there were any people inside the earth. 'By no means,' I replied. This gave me an opportunity to speak of how God created the universe. He commented, 'I was taught that we live in a house with many rooms. Our life is just a passing through one of these rooms. It is a long pilgrimage. But if what you say is true, then this whole idea of the rooms may be wrong. Who knows? There may be no gods. But what you say brings darkness to me. I am confused.'

"I replied to him, 'I see what you mean. If there is no God, then it is dark. But since God does exist and is truth, it is not dark if we have eyes to see. God has made Himself known. The light of the knowledge of God shines, not in the sky, but in the face of the man named Jesus Christ.'

"He asked me to tell him more, and so, as we traveled on,

I unfolded the story. He was distressed with the story of Jesus' sufferings, but when I spoke of his rising from the grave and ascending into heaven, the lama exclaimed, 'He must be a god! He must be a god!' Since he traveled another route, that was my last opportunity to discuss this with him. I'm so glad though that I could share briefly and in a friendly way with this Tibetan. He certainly had an open mind!"

"I wish that I understood better what they are thinking," I responded. "Sometimes down there on the street the monks mimic right back to me what I have laboriously said in the chapel, hand motions and all! I sometimes think they reckon our God is not as powerful as we say he is!"

Paul and Fred were intrigued as we told them that Lozongdrema, the helper who came with us from Batang, sometimes shared with Betty the old wives' tales which she had been hearing from childhood, stories of the strange and unusual. When she had free time, she would visit other people from Batang. They welcomed her, and no doubt they asked her some questions about us foreigners. As she spent more and more of her leisure with these cronies, we began to notice that instead of this being a help to her, she seemed more restless and unsure of herself than we had ever seen her. Nor for a while could we determine what the matter was or how best Betty could counsel her. One day, her fingers playing nervously with her black apron, she opened up. "My friends in the caravansary tell me scary stories about demons and spirits. They told me how a demon had possessed a man they knew, forcing him out of bed. He didn't have time to dress properly before they made him run off as fast as the wind. Even faster than the wind, they said! Do you think that could be true?"

"Some stories the more they are told, the bigger they get," Betty countered. "But I do not doubt that evil spirits exist and are always harmful. When a person allows himself to become the servant of an evil spirit, he will suffer as a result. Evil spirits can be sent away by the true God, and they are afraid of him. You can ask God to protect you. You know how often I have told you that he loves you so much that he has sent Jesus here to save you."

Betty went on to describe the problem she had going over the catechism with Lozongdrema. The catechism says something about God never having been born and never dying. When she asked her, "Will God die?" she answered, "Oh, yes!" Puzzled, Betty replied, "Why?" And Lozongdrema said, "Oh, he will die for the sins of the world."

"I've got my work cut out for me," Betty exclaimed. "Well, anyway, I did ask Lozongdrema if she didn't have some younger women she could spend her time with."

"I don't have many other friends," she replied. "And there is only one large room, so we all have to be together around the fire. The younger women like to hear these stories, but we're afraid when we have to go home in the dark."

Paul and Fred had listened intently. I spoke up, saying, "It will take a miracle to have a breakthrough among Tibetans, but that's what we're asking God for." Our visitors encouraged us to continue to trust God to see multiplied conversions and strong Christian growth to this end.

The beginning of that miracle was just then unfolding. God brought a Chinese evangelist, John Ding, to our city as the Chinese New Year's festivities were about to begin. John had come with a strong call to share Jesus with Tibetans after leaving a good government job. Word of his outstanding ministry in Chengdu had preceded him, and now the China Inland Mission invited him to use their chapel for special meetings during the holidays. He consented but asked the small group of believers to back him up with faith for a great work of the Holy Spirit. Out of desperation and the hope he kindled, we all agreed.

Chinese New Year's on the Tibetan border was a two week vacation from business, offices, and schools, with continuous feasts, games, and street displays. The Tibetans would have their New Year celebrations a month later, but they enjoyed this excitement, too. The dragon dancers, the stilt walkers, the brightly-dressed men wearing paper horses or boats around their waists! The firecrackers and the incessant clatter of cymbals and gongs! Yet that was not all.

Alongside these festivities in 1948 a quiet, dramatic work started in the chapel as this Shanghai-born John Ding shared his own encounter with God, and how his repentance and faith in Christ had wonderfully changed his life. He urged the hearers to accept the same God-given opportunity for forgiveness and the assurance of eternal life with God. He spoke vividly of the moral failures which bind us and from which God can free us. Listeners leaned forward intently, and then many of them responded. Never before had there been such a harvest in this place. Over fifty people, Chinese and some Tibetans, confessed their faith in Christ. What started as special meetings turned into a spiritual movement which rocked us all.

This kind of breakthrough was totally unprecedented here. In a place where you could have counted the converts on the fingers of two hands, suddenly we saw a full house. And something else was going on in the homes of Christians as gradually ordinary conversation turned into conversational prayer. We would say to one another, "Let's talk to God about this." And then prayer flowed with an ease and assurance which gripped us mightily. It was person to person, awareness of God's desire and intention to bring Tibetans to himself in spite of all seeming barriers. In a fresh, new way we sensed that our lives were "in the Spirit" and that thus equipped, God's blessing was going to flow to a degree we had never before anticipated or seen. And it did spread to other places in eastern Tibet.

Around that time I was walking up the river road and caught up with three Tibetan pilgrims, a lama and two

monks. They all had packs on their backs and each held in
his hand a long bamboo pole with a spearhead on top and
small prayer flags below it. These men had been on pilgrimage and were now returning to a place near Ganzi to the
North. The lama and his companions were willing to listen
to me say, "I want to come to Ganzi to tell people about the
holy God who loves each one of us. He sent our Savior to
free us from sin. This Savior defeated all devils by taking
our sins away as far as the East is from the West. The Savior
did this by defeating death. He died by accepting all the
punishment for the sin of the world and then came alive
again. Then he went back to heaven, saying that if we would
believe in him, he would come back for us at the end of this
life and take us to be with God in heaven forever. This
Savior's name is Jesus, and he does for us what we never
can do for ourselves. He gives us his Spirit, and his Spirit
brings us heavenly life."

Puzzled he asked me, "Does Jesus live in heaven?" I
replied, "Yes, he lives in heaven, but he also lives in my
heart and in the heart of anyone willing to receive him as
Savior and Lord." It was a brief opportunity I had, but in a
special way with Tibetans I felt God's hand timing and
arranging a significant open door for me in giving them
each a Gospel portion, which they gladly received, we said
our farewells. Our prayers would follow them.

Soon after this I received belated word of my mother's
step into heavenly places. She had heard of the birth of our
daughter and her namesake, Marion, expressing a wish that
she had the strength to knit a sweater for her. A cousin got
to work and did this in place of my mother.

After John Ding's meetings I had the privilege of
baptizing three Tibetans who had placed their faith in
Christ: Lozongdrema, our cook Ahnu, and a young man,
Mako. The cook was so altered in her brash attitudes and
her cooking that we proclaimed to one another that she now

produced "saved pancakes"!

For Lozongdrema demonic forces put up a struggle and a fresh challenge to our faith. One evening we heard noise downstairs, a thumping and groaning which brought us all down the narrow stairs. To our surprise we discovered Lozongdrema acting as though attacked by evil spirits. She rammed her head repeatedly against the wall. She seemed unaware of our presence, but we felt the presence of something else very evil. As we prayed she quieted down. When she was normal again, Margaret counseled with her about her need to trust wholly in Christ and reject all attempts of the devil to reassert any claim on her life. Lozongdrema was so glad to be delivered from her experience that she promised to do just that. Mako had a quieter, deeper transition. His reaction to meeting and accepting Christ was that of a "hunger and thirst after righteousness."

John Ding, the evangelist, fully occupied with caring for new believers and continuing to preach at the chapel found his ministry interrupted in a most unusual way. "The Lord has told me to go all the way back to Shanghai and put something right," he said. "After preaching to others about sin, I have been convicted by the Lord about 20 silver dollars which I unfairly got from two friends when I was 13 years old. The Lord has instructed me to go find them, confess my lies, and make restitution. How can I do less than that which I urge other people to do – to get right with God and with any whom we have wronged?" His demonstration of humble obedience probably accomplished more than many sermons. He walked away from what some would call his personal success, asked others to carry on the instruction of new believers, and started across China without the funds for the trip. On the first leg of this trip he came to a flooded river, impossible to cross. Travelers were squatting hopelessly on the bank. "What do you want me to do now, Lord?" he prayed silently. "Step down into the water," came the answer, and John did just that. As he stood in the water, it began to drop. Sensing what was happening, he reached back for a small child and placed him on his shoulders. Beckoning to the others to follow him, he began to cross. And the river was shallow enough to wade through. As soon as they all got safely to the other side, the water rose back to its previous flood level. Then at the first city he reached a Christian doctor asked him if he would hand carry a microscope from Shanghai back to his hospital, thus supplying him with the travel funds he needed. He put things right in Shanghai and before long returned to Kangding rejoicing.

The Tibetan monastery five minutes up the street from our house held 15 large prayer wheels. Its prayer hall in the main building at the back rumbled with the chanting of its monks. I often thought of these pathetic human endeavors as well as the fact that God is not silent. He is speaking on the first page of the Bible, and He is speaking on the last page. And His Holy Spirit is our personal guide day by day. How God in His great love must yearn for Tibetans, both men and women, to come into the freedom and delight of a personal relationship with Him. We were gripped with fresh hope for our witness to Tibetans and a spirit of believing prayer, based on God's own great love for them.

In a caravansary where a priest seeks to drive out evil spirits from a sick person, he dances in a fearsome mask, wearing an apron with the picture of a skull on it, he swirls burning incense in sweeping motions all the way out to the gates. Thus he portrays what he thinks is his cleansing of the patient and the exorcism of all evil spirits.

Mako and I visited such a caravansary in the city and sat with a merchant monk as he slips one yellow bead after another through his fingers. Lay people would use brown or black rosaries. He has yellow tapes tying up his boots. They would use varicolored tapes. "It is our custom!" he tells me, breaking into his repetition of the prayer, "O mani padme hum."

"God, whom I worship, declares in His holy Word that repeated prayers are useless," I say, "For He hears us the first time we pray."

"But it is our custom," he persists, scratching his shaven head.

I smiled. "In the past you have changed your religion and customs. Your Buddhism is an import from India, but the Holy God is no import. He has been here in Tibet since before the beginning of time. He is the Creator of heaven and earth, and we all are his creatures. He is here with us now. Customs vary because they are made by man. Truth does not vary, because it comes from the unchanging Holy God. For example, He says that it is wrong to lie. It is wrong to lie in my country, and it is wrong to lie in your country because that is God's universal truth. Truth is more powerful than custom. The wonderful truth about God is that He loves you and wants to help you and He has helped me."

After a few moments the monk says, "I've heard this in your chapel. I don't need your Savior." The beads flow faster through his hand. There is resistance here.

I know it is time to move on. "I must go now," I say. "Thank you for letting us rest here for a while, and thank you for the bowl of butter tea. You are so kind."

"Go slowly!" he says, and I reply, "Sit slowly."

Those traditional farewells are typical of an ancient pattern of life, and actually are similar to Chinese courtesies with their "man-man-dzo" or "go slowly". Slow or fast, I trust that this worldly merchant, so occupied with profitable commerce, may wonder how he can secure the satisfaction Mako and I possess. "Mako", I say, "Jesus will still knock at the door of his heart."

As the two of us walk down the street Mako speaks up, saying to me, "My parents in Batang expected me to be a monk. My father was the town crier. I used to follow him around, very proud of his loud voice as the people looked out doors and windows, listening to his announcements. Now I want to be like John the Baptist, telling people about Jesus and how he saves us from sin and gives us eternal life."

We had that opportunity a few minutes later when some Tibetans, resting beside the cobbled street welcomed us in a warm conversation.

CHAPTER 12

HANDLING A TIBETAN DISPUTE

It was a lazy afternoon on the road in eastern Tibet. Certainly I had earned a rest after a cold four-o'clock start that morning, a climb up and over the pass, and now the inviting warmth of the sun at the caravan campsite. I was traveling with a fast caravan of horses and mules, and several of the Khamba drivers had taken the animals out to graze. What was left were twelve separate stacks of loads spaced around a large circle, and a number of wispy campfires beside several of them.

From where I lay resting on my saddle rugs, my head propped up against a load, I could hear the rippling of the stream which split and ran on both sides of us before meeting again below us. Down the valley and some distance away sat a Tibetan farmhouse, squat and secure, surrounded by a ripening field of barley, the valley sides beyond and a glistening snow peak in the distance.

The grass around me crested with wild flowers. It was the month of August. Here at 10,000 feet altitude the summer was short. It was good to sip butter tea and soak up the sunshine. How comfortable I felt! Altitudes like this posed no problem to me, which I couldn't say of the monastery town of Litang at 14,000 feet where I had found myself sometimes breathing hard.

Norje, my swarthy, heavy-set helper, crouched by the fire he had built and pulled the embers closer together. He was an old hand in the tea trade, thoroughly familiar with life on the road. Lifting his shaven head, he looked at me and said, "I was with a caravan once on this road, and we were followed by bandits for days. We would catch sight of them from time to time, scouting us from far off." He mused at the memory.

"How did you protect yourself?" I asked him, sensing a good story.

"Really we had no sure protection," he answered. "We divided up by threes along the whole route of our yak train, knowing that any three of us could be ambushed and killed outright by those men. But at least we reckoned that the sound of shots would warn all the rest in time to seek cover. The plan worked. Those bandits could see we were alert, and they never attacked. Other caravans haven't been so fortunate."

I asked him about bandits, and he snorted, "Farmers in season; bandits out of season. That's what they are!"

"But you are a draba, aren't you? You're safe from attack because you are a priest!"

"I used to be a priest," he corrected me, "but then I broke my vows. After years of keeping the rules, I met a pretty girl and broke my promises of celibacy. It was as simple as that. Later I was invited back to the monastery. Actually I live there some of the time, but I am not allowed to join in the chanting services. No, I just spend my time trading for the abbot. Though my head is shaved, I receive no respect from either monks or laymen now."

Suddenly we heard hoof beats and looked up. Was this

another caravan or was it visitors? Often people would come for medicine when the word spread that a foreigner was passing by. No, it was just Yeshe, the cheerful driver who was responsible for our small party's animals. He was bringing our horses in, a bit early I thought to myself. But he didn't tether them, leaving them to graze close by. Yeshe glanced our way, then rode over to our campfire and slipped to the ground. His face was a study of concern. "Some of the horses belonging to other members of the caravan are lost and probably taken by local farmers," he announced, and then he hastened to say, "None of ours! I kept watch on them. I've got to go right over and tell Losang what's happened." He leaped on his horse, gave a slap on its rump, and it trotted across the open field to where Losang, the caravan leader, was located. We watched Yeshe break the news to him, while several other men gathered closely around. Then three of them went for some nearby horses, their rifles slung conspicuously over their backs as they rode off down the valley. Since one of them had borrowed Yeshe's horse, he slowly plodded back to us in his clumsy, thin-soled boots. Lowering himself to the ground, he sat there cross-legged and pulled out his tea bowl from the depths of his sheepskin robe.

"Tell us what's up", demanded Norje impatiently as he filled the bowl.

"I'm not sure, but it could be big trouble," Yeshe replied. Then he explained, "Some of the men dozed off instead of keeping an eye on the animals. When they woke up, they couldn't find their horses anywhere, but they saw where they had broken into some fields of grain. You know how angry that would make the farmers. So the other men sent me back here. Now Losang has gone to see what he can do about it." He pulled his big braid with red wool woven into it tighter around his head and sipped some tea. Then he rubbed his chin meditatively.

A while later Losang and his friends rode back into camp, stopping first by our campfire. He looked tense and grim. "We've lost eighteen horses," he told us. "We found the farmers that rounded them up. They have them penned up in the stables under one of the houses down the valley, and they're guarding them there." He stopped to sniff up some snuff from a small container.

And then he addressed me directly, "I need your help. I want you to go over and talk to the farmers for us."

"And what would I say?" was my surprised response.

"You will think of something," he replied. "They curse us. They threaten to make us pay a quarter brick of tea for each three strides one of our horses made into a field. That's outrageous! You can help us bargain with them."

"But who am I for them to listen to me?" I asked.

Losang laughed an answered, "You're a foreigner, and you know the Chinese magistrate. All you need to do is threaten that you'll report them to him, and they'll back off."

"But I've only met the magistrate once or twice. I hardly know him," I objected.

"These farmers don't know that," Losang said confidently. "Come, we've got to deal with this quickly before they have time to think up more problems."

I could understand the sense of that, and I knew that if we didn't settle this matter, we would probably be delayed a day on the road. But I wasn't prepared to bluster and threaten in the way I knew Losang wanted me to do.

A man brought over my horse, put on the bridle and saddle, and offered it to me. Norje urged me to mount as he held its head. "I'll do what I can do," I said to Losang, "but I don't know what to say. And I'd like to see first how much damage the horses did." With that I swung up easily into my saddle, and we started off.

This time we were a group of eight, and all the Tibetans were armed with an assortment of old rifles. They seemed in remarkable good humor. After all, the day was turning out to be anything but routine. Losang leaned over in his saddle toward me and said with a trace of a smirk, "We travel together, so we are all friends! Is that not so?"

"La-so, la-so — Yes, yes", I guardedly admitted. I knew that I did face an obligation that I was expected to fulfill, but I was exceedingly surprised to become a major player. It is one thing to help spontaneously, doing what you know how to do, but it is quite another matter to be led into a cross-cultural maze. I tried to gather my thoughts and remember bits and fragments of conversations I had heard. I knew that farmers on the trade route disliked the passing caravans because of their frequent depredations. The crops were too precious for them to suffer this lightly. I knew that the drivers were often careless and rude to them. Undoubtedly those farmers down the road wanted to settle old scores and were now congratulating themselves on being in a strong bargaining position. So I was supposed to persuade them to relent and let our animals go free at little cost to an offending caravan? Not a chance!

I was particularly interested to inspect the fields damaged by the horses. Some spots had obviously been badly trampled down. I pointed this out to Losang, saying with a shake of my head, "The farmers deserve something for that loss."

"It's not much," he said blandly, "nothing much!" He gave me a speculative glance to see whether I had bought into what he had just said. For my part I was asking the Lord to undertake in this strange situation that I found myself in.

At last we approached the farmhouse where the horses were being held. Like most Tibetans dwellings it looked like a fort with its solid bulk and narrow windows high above. Several armed men stood on watch at the double doors at the front. This wasn't going to be a pushover!

Losang, deciding on a bluff, rode up by himself to the

entrance and demanded the right to enter and count the animals. The farmers in their sheepskins were unimpressed and rebuffed him "Nobody gets in until we talk," was their reply.

By this time some of Losang's companions drew up behind him. They dismounted and began to curse and shout at the guards. Tempers were rising, and a bit of shoving commenced. Then Losang gave a command and his men backed off. The two groups began to parley across the space of the eight to ten feet separating them. I was standing by my horse some thirty feet away. A cool breeze made me glad that I had slipped on my sheepskin jacket. Ever so often the farmers would glance my way, well aware that I was that rare species, a "piling" or foreigner.

When at last Norje strode back up to me, he announced that the farmers had agreed to let me go inside for a check on the number of captured horses in their possession. They wouldn't allow any one else from our party, however, to accompany me. When I slowly approached the gate and dismounted, the guards called to someone inside, and the wooden bolt slid noisily inside. Then one door of the double gate swung open, and I was invited to step inside.

Coming in from the sunshine, I was blinded, yet I sensed and heard people around me. They jostled up close to get a good look at this stranger from the outside world. Even when my eyes began to adjust to the dim light, it was too dark for me to see much. A farmer sensibly lit a piece of fat pine and with this as a torch led me around the ground floor stables. He pointed the animals out, one by one, and I kept count with him. "Fifteen, sixteen, seventeen, and, yes, eighteen." They were all accounted for, stabled on one side, while some of the farmers' horses were over on the other side.

I turned to go outside, but one of the farmers detained me. "We are within our rights," he argued. "These horses did a lot of damage to our grain, and we won't release them until we are paid forty bricks of tea."

Shaking my head, I said, "You know that is too much, and I, even though a foreigner, know it is too much." At my reply others chimed in with discussion, but I pushed myself through the crowd toward the doors. "I'll talk it over," I said. Up a slope I rode to where my caravan men were gathered. They hailed me, eager to discover what I would report. After we drew together in a huddle, I told them of my findings and particularly the latter part of my conversation I had had with the farmers – their demands and my response.

"They do have some valid complaints," I said. "They say that every week of the summer season they have problems like this with passing caravans. And they claim that you men act as though they were just growing grain to fatten your animals. They say that you wouldn't act the same way if you were closer to a large town. That you would be more careful there! I think that you are going to have to pay something."

My companions did not dispute what I said. They were disappointed but knew that I had objected to a high penalty. Losang nodded and said, "We'll talk with the farmers again." Once more I distanced myself from their palaver, but after a while they came back. Losang looked a little flustered. "We shouldn't pay more than two bricks," he declared and grasped his short sword. But he cooled down and began to whisper with his assistant. Then he straightened up and came over to me. "There's only one way to settle this," he said. "You will have to be the judge."

"What?" I rejoined, "That's impossible. How could I decide the damage payment? I don't know enough about your Kham country custom and penalties."

He didn't answer me but instead turned and called down to the guards at the gate, "We offer this foreigner to judge the matter. Is this acceptable to you?" They went inside to consult with their confederates, and then one of them came out and shouted, "We agree that he can be the judge."

Losang had neatly passed the decision to me, and I was perplexed. The possibilities for error were so great! If I pleased one side, would the other side wish be angry? How was I to decide what penalty measured in tea would reach that delicate balance that would satisfy both sides? And if I refused to help? No, that was unthinkable, too. I simply had to have divine guidance.

I walked slowly toward the gate to be met by a spokesman for the farmers. He was youngish but weather-beaten as his sheepskin. He looked me over with a steady, penetrating stare. What did he see in me that would give him any trust in my reckoning?

"Whatever you say, that will be it," he told me with a blank look on his face.

I wouldn't have long to come up with a figure. I looked around me. My men had clustered behind me "Why, they're enjoying this!" I thought to myself, "They want to see how the foreigner will figure this out." I spurred myself to make a decision. With a brief prayer for help, I took a deep breath. This was it! "For the damage done by the caravan horses in the fields I say that Losang shall pay a total of six bricks of tea," I pronounced. And I turned and without looking back walked away and over to my horse.

There were a few intense moments of silence before the gates creaked open. Next, the horses appeared, one after another, the farmers slapping their flanks to hurry them along. Our men began counting them and shooing them off in the direction of our camp site. Then what a hullabaloo as everybody, caravan men and farmers, began to mount and start after the loose animals.

My ordeal was not over. I soon found myself surrounded by our men pleading, "Make it lower! Make it lower!" on one side and the farmers, brushing against my leg, pressing in and telling me to "Make it higher! Make it higher!" on the other side. I turned my head from one side, saying repeatedly, "That's it! What I have said I have said."

The climax came later by Losang's campfire as his men solemnly opened a load of tea. Slowly and carefully they broke through the woven basket cover to get at six bricks of tea. From my campfire I saw our men talking emphatically, as the farmers inspected the bricks of tea, then placed them in their baggy robes. Seemingly satisfied, they said a dignified farewell, mounted, and rose off down the valley. Our camp was quiet once more, and the crisis past.

Losang seemed in a good mood, and the other men also appeared content. I was glad for that, but still I thought it a little strange. Back at my own campfire I asked Norje pointblank how he thought the matter stood. After all, I had caused them to pay a substantial fine to the farmers.

The men appeared content.

Then he enlightened me. "Oh, yes," he said. "Everything turned out well. You set a fair amount, but you neglected to specify what grade of tea should be paid over. Our men knew where they had some very coarse tea. These farmers hardly know the difference because they are used to drinking poor tea all the time. So they didn't object, and Losang gets off without paying too much. This way everybody is happy."

He stirred the soggy dumplings in the pot, and though I knew they would be heavy I felt my appetite rise. I'd passed some sort of test. And what a story it would make for Tibetans at many a hearth and campfire, in its various versions, of course! It would depend on whether the farmers were telling it or the caravan men.

I mused about the confidence Losang had that he could work out a solution by using me. How did he dare place his affairs in my hands? I had no way except to place my trust in God, so I was grateful that my Lord had rescued me. Justice, Kham-style justice, had been served. I had just learned an unusual lesson in deliverance. Hmm! That stew smelled delicious. I handed over my bowl for Norje to fill. And holding it once again, I gave thanks to God for guiding me through a difficult challenge.

He was also leading me into being on the lookout for people with problems as an opportunity to offer to pray for them and the solution of their problems. That confidence is based on God the Creator, who talks to us and listens to us with loving concern.

CHAPTER 13

A TIME TO MOVE

Tibetans love horse races, and a famous race takes place each year on Run Horse Mountain which towers over the city of Kangding. The legend is that the god of the mountain became angry with the people living there and let loose an avalanche which buried them. We could still see the boulder strewn plain where the old city once stood. The race was then established by those who honored this god and as a precaution against being wiped out by his anger again.

We were experiencing daily another type of race, a race to keep up with the decreasing value of Chinese paper money. Tibetans no longer wanted to be paid in it. They demanded silver, either Chinese dollars or the Tibetan coins called rupees. One day a girl who had sold us eggs came back to us weeping. Her mother had beaten her because the amount we had paid her in paper currency halved in value overnight. We gave her the difference, and she dried her tears on the corner of her apron. A little while later she returned with the money in her hand and said, "My mother doesn't want paper money. She says you must pay her in rice." The mother must have figured us out for a soft touch, but we went ahead and measured out some rice, giving it to the girl instead of paper money.

Here's the record. In the first two months after we arrived from Batang, bread tripled in price. In the month of October, 1947, prices doubled while the foreign exchange rate only increased a tenth. Edie neglected to withdraw the equivalent of $35 from the bank over a period of five months, and by then it was worth $4. By December the ingredients for our homemade bread were costing fifty cents a loaf, and this was in 1947 dollars. When we took our baby, Marion, down to Chengdu in March for a medical checkup, her bill for a one week stay, not involving any meals, was one million dollars Chinese! With justification we called her our "million dollar baby". We were in a race for survivalists, not for those easily discouraged, and this race involved everybody around us.

From birth Marion had had a rattling sound in her chest which disturbed us. The French doctor recommended that we take her down to Chengdu for tests, and we left at the beginning of March, 1948, when she was only six weeks old. We traveled by "chair", exposed to the winds. Betty sat with a blanket around her shoulders and wrapped over the baby in her lap. That afternoon as we turned south on the Dong River, we got into quite a sandstorm. For a while it was like crossing a desert. The sand was up to the men's ankles, and the wind so strong that at times it made them stop in their tracks. One woman carrying a load of wood on her back was simply blown right over. Nevertheless, we reached the river crossing at Luding, where we spent the night in an inn. Betty and I were pleased with our carriers, but our companions, Edie and Ahnu, had carriers who, due to opium smoking continually, dragged in late. The next day we spent climbing Two Wolf Mountain, at first warmed by the sun but then higher up experiencing bitter cold. A small blizzard was blowing snow right into our faces, and we hurried into a shack near the top of the pass where we would spend the night. Never mind the half dozen adults and three noisy children jammed with us in one small room. The charcoal fire and hot tea soon warmed us up. Betty felt Marion's cheek, and she was warm as toast and cooing with delight.

In the morning we woke to a world transformed by deep snow. It was a breathtaking sight. The wind had driven the snow at every post, bush, or tree, leaving it there in streamlined shapes. On the far side of the pass we found the snow even deeper, covering the pathway, hiding the ice on the stone steps, and concealing the drop-offs at the side. One of Edie's carriers hurt his foot so she had to walk. One of Ahnu's carriers fell down, so she decided to walk as well. Then Betty thought she better try walking. Giving me Marion to carry, she edged along, helped by a young Chinese soldier in front and one of her carriers from behind. It was too slippery for her, and the carrier insisted she get back in the chair. He pointed to the cleats on his sandals, and she understood. She was nervous, however, about carrying Marion with her in the chair.

The soldier then came over to me and said, "Let me carry the child because I have straw sandals." He was soon ahead of us and out of sight. We were very trustful of many traveling companions if we had been able to size them up. Marion would be all right. I had my work cut out just taking care of myself in the slippery descent.

I had no choice but to slide on the path. What I wanted to avoid was a bad fall. I grasped for branches and roots as handholds. On one steep incline a heavy-set merchant ahead of me lost his balance, fell, bumped into Ahnu, and they both landed at the turn below in an ignominious heap. When we all reached the bottom of the pass and the open road, the young soldier was waiting for us, sitting on a rock, cradling our baby in his arms. Betty thanked him heartily and took her back.

Two days later I was buying bus tickets in Yaan for the

ride to Chengdu. Betty had instructed me to be sure and get low numbers in order for us to sit at the front. The next morning at the bus station we discovered that our family tickets – 2, 7, and 9 – were in the last two rows of the bus. Betty was appalled at the tight leg room back there, but the conductor raised his arms helplessly. Then the merchant who had bumped into Ahnu on the pass got up and exchanged his front row seat with Betty. Such courtesy, and we still remember it with deep respect! When the doctors in Chengdu were unable to suggest anything for Marion and told us she would outgrow the rattling sound with time, we were disappointed. More immediate help came from a young pharmacist from England named Gordon Bell, who was waiting in Chengdu en route to Kangding for Tibetan work. He ventured his opinion to us regarding Marion's chest by saying, "I've got a specific for that condition. Would you like me to try it?" When he explained that he carried a stock of homeopathic medicine, we were a trifle hesitant. He told us she would not be in any danger, so we agreed for him to try his medicine on her. It worked a complete cure on Marion in 24 hours, our one experience with homeopathy.

Gordon Bell, and his companion, Geoffrey Bull, came with us on the return trip to Kangding. Geoff carried Marion up the snowy pass of Two Wolf Mountain. Part way up I spotted a tea carrier who had lost his balance and fallen off the steep path with his load strapped to him. Now spread-eagled in the snow, he lay dazed and helpless. He was injured and bleeding profusely. Other carriers had passed him, not daring to try and help him. Several of us travelers unfastened his load and lifted it off. The man had a bad gash that reached right to the edge of one eye. Betty took charge, cleaning up and dressing his wound. She was concerned about his getting further treatment in Kangding, so she explained where the hospital was. "I can make it," he said, and he looked young and fit enough to do so. We had to continue on our way but had the satisfaction of seeing him begin to climb slowly after us.

In view of the deteriorating political situation we had observed, we felt that our party must begin its preparations and move soon to Ganzi or lose that opportunity entirely. This Tibetan town and large monastery is on the northwest road, the alternate to the route through Batang and on to Chamdo and Lhasa. In southeastern Tibet, which is called Kham, the rivers and mountain ranges run mostly from north to south. Since Batang is due west of Kangding, this terrain is mostly an up and down washboard except for some plateaus. While the road westward through Batang is shorter, the northern road arcs toward the west, following easier river valleys and fewer high passes. Consequently it is a far more traveled route.

Foreign friends in Kangding tried to dissuade us from even considering living in Ganzi. It had been visited briefly by a number of foreigners, but no one as yet had tried to settle there. "You won't be able to get enough food to survive in such a place," was the warning. Betty and I had vivid memories of the problems we had had in Batang to get provisions, but we believed this would be different. First of all, we would plan to take an ample stock of commercial goods, of foodstuffs, and of the local silver currency, an old Chinese coin smaller than the more common Chinese silver dollar. Also we expected to generate some income when we conducted our clinic. Was this plan feasible? We broached it to the Tibetans who would accompany us, and they couldn't visualize any difficulty at all.

Lozongdrema was willing to accompany us, for since the death of her mother she had no relatives in Batang. We asked an older woman, Drashi, to join us, and she accepted. Then we had Mako, the young man from Batang, who was proving out very well as an aide at the Catholic hospital. He would assist Hester and Edie with the dispensary we projected. Mako had told me about his father, a farmer and the town crier. As a boy Mako wanted to attend school. At this point some Batang Christians persuaded his father to let him be a student. Mako was grateful to them for helping him when the course of his life hung in the balance, and that was the beginning of his awareness of what Christians believed.

In one of our conversations Mako made a surprising admission, telling me, "I knew Lozongdrema in Batang. I remember going to her house to buy vegetables." He hesitated and then flushed before saying, "I had a feeling about her that I can't express to you." By this time I had gathered that he was interested in her, and he went on to say that he wanted to marry her. When she was receptive to his proposal, the local church in Kangding put on a reception for the young couple. She dressed as usual in Tibetan clothes, new ones for the occasion, her hair braided. Her broad face, rosy cheeks, and bright eyes made her a beauty, but she was also very shy. Mako still wore a Chinese gown. He was short and slight, his manner calm and gentle. Would his education and her lack of schooling be a problem? They did have their faith in common.

"Would your family approve of this match?" I had asked Mako, and he assured me they did. He called the skinners to prepare our loads for the anticipated trip. As I watched them sewing up the wet skins around our boxes, I was impressed again with their speed. And I noted that they stuck a short stick through the skin on both sides of each load. To this they attached leather thongs. "Why do they do that?" I asked Mako, "I never saw anything like that on the loads on the Batang road."

"The caravans on the Ganzi road use another custom," he replied, "You can tell where goods are going by whether they have sticks on the side or not. As you know, on the Batang road the leather thongs are on the pack saddles. This is another custom."

Well, why not? The Tibetan province of Kham has 39 different tribes, and we could expect some variety in their speech and customs. One of the peculiarities was that from region to region they favored this issue of silver rupee or that one. "I can't see any difference, Mako" I would say. "Oh, yes there is," he would reply. "See the way that leaf is turned, and here the line of the mouth is turned up instead of down." Gradually I saw what he was pointing at, but it took me some time to identify the slight differences.

A skin covered load in Ganzi.

We paid the skinners in brick tea. If it had been silver dollars, we would have gone through the careful process of their ringing each one to see if it rang true. I discovered a firm in the city that would receive, store, and forward tea according to my instructions, and this would be our bank in the future. Paper money was worthless beyond Kangding, and it was going out of style in the city itself. Banks couldn't bring in loads of new currency fast enough to keep up with the inflation. We were reaching a barter stage. Meanwhile, the merchants made money on the shifting commodities market. This week rice was a bargain, next week tea. My double entry bookkeeping began to have some new accounts. I recall one time we put all our cash into Chinese noodles, and then when we had a shortage we could eat our reserves. And once we did that until we couldn't face eating any more noodles!

Frequently mule caravans would file right past our house and up the alley behind it to a storehouse. First, we would hear the jingle of mule bells. The lead mule would usually have a yak tail, dyed red, hung below his neck as well as a big bell. His bridle would include a bright-colored pad against his forehead, usually with a mirror attached to it. That supposedly would scare off any evil spirits, for these would be frightened to see themselves!

The caravan Tibetans in their sheepskins would whistle to their watchdogs to keep them away from yapping city curs. The loads were sometimes wool and dried skins. Incoming tea from Yaan might come on the backs of Yunnan ponies instead of men. The brick tea bundles were dumped in the alley and then carried into the storehouse. Because of lack of space some tea loads were covered with skin out in the alley and left right there to dry, smell and all. They would be stacked up later in the compound, and when we left, carriers would take them out of the city to where yak were. Out there the animals could graze a little while waiting.

It was almost business as usual for Tibetan traders, but we had a sense of urgency. We had heard enough in

Chengdu to realize that the campuses were hotbeds of unrest and financial struggle. The students were asking the government to deal with corruption. If they had seen some signs of willingness to remedy such abuses, they might have responded favorably. But the face presented by Communism in its propaganda was that of righteousness and concern for the common people. Who could object to that? Especially when the national government seemed unable to stem inflation. Students were going hungry because their small resources were being wiped out. It was easy to blame the government for their hardships. And the government wrestled unsuccessfully with its bloated bureaucracy and recalcitrant provincial warlords.

Aware of the worsening situation, wouldn't we have been better off to head for the coast instead of planning to go even deeper into the interior? Not necessarily! Up to this point many foreigners were seeking to dodge and keep out of the reach of hostilities, convinced that if Communism took over we might be able to make ourselves useful enough so that we would be allowed to stay in China. And for those of us up in eastern Tibet there was still the thought that as a last resort we might try to cross the border beyond Batang and Derge into central Tibet, headed for India. The Tibetan government might take a more lenient view toward us if we were in transit as refugees.

We were waiting for a caravan to Ganzi that could take our 98 loads when we received the offer of some horses in an express caravan. This would not be slowed down by yak. Such a caravan would take 14 to 18 days in comparison to the 25-27 days a yak caravan would require to reach Ganzi. Mailmen, working in relays delivered letters there in 10 days. We debated the pros and cons of splitting up in two parties. I urged Margaret, Edie and Hester to go ahead with this fast caravan, knowing that Margaret and Edie had already made one trip into the grasslands and knew what travel on the road was like. We could send Mako and Drashi with them and on arrival Mako would help them find temporary lodging and begin to look for a place for us to stay as well, hopefully before Betty and I arrived with the heavier loads.

We had a covered basket made for our baby, and we located a man who was willing to carry this all the way on his back. Lozongdrema would accompany us as well. We all agreed to this plan, so the first party rode off on July 23, 1948. We already had our yak caravan lined up and left five days later, heartily grateful that one more long trip preparation was over. Our team was on its way to establish the first new station in northern Kham in forty years.

CHAPTER 14

A NEW STATION IN GANZI

🌺

For weeks the skin-bound boxes had been stacked up behind the chapel, sheltered under the eaves. They ranged in size from compact bundles of brick tea to steamer trunks and even a folding organ. The day came when the tea carriers swarmed in and began to load up for the haul to the caravan camp grounds outside the city gate. There were so many of them, and they moved so swiftly that I gave up trying to keep track of the loads. They knew their job and required no help from me.

Later I walked out of the city to the spot where our loads were being dumped and talked to two of the Tibetans there. "Those two boxes are our food boxes," I pointed out. "Their lids open up. See the padlocks? We'll need them handy every day, so be sure you have them where we can get at them." They assured me that those boxes would always be available. "Oh, and one other thing," I said, "See that large box with white markers on it? It's heavy, but I don't want it to get wet. Be sure and stack it off the ground." Again they agreed, "La-so, la-so! Yes, yes!"

What then was our dismay the first night out on the road to discover that we were traveling with only half of the caravan and that our food boxes had been left behind for a second group of yak to bring! The leader of our yak drivers was quite unconcerned. "They will catch up with us in two or three days," he promised. "And if you run out of food, you can borrow some from us."

When I brought this word back to Betty and Lozongdrema, they were shocked. "All the work we did to have everything we needed!" said Betty. "Those fresh eggs buried in the flour bag! Well, that means our well-planned menus go out the window until those boxes show up. Next time we don't take anything for granted!"

We had to wait until the eighth day before we met with the other half of the caravan and received our food boxes. We had managed in the meantime with what we happened to have in our saddlebags and some butter we borrowed from the caravan men. As for the heavy organ box, more often than not I found it sitting on damp ground at the bottom of a pile. We were learning what to expect. It was something else again to know when to insist on our rights, when to let something slide by without comment, and how to anticipate these carefree men with their established routines.

Each day we lifted Marion into the open end of her basket and tucked her in. Then the carrier placed the straps over his shoulders and was ready to start off. He used his large umbrella as a walking stick in the early mornings and then raised it to shield Marion from the sun later in the day. That umbrella made it easy for us to spot him and his small human cargo. The pace of his walking would lull Marion to sleep, but around feeding, time we listened for the little wail that would signal us to call for a stop. After a break like that we four would be behind the others and then gradually we would pass group after group of slow moving yak. They were broken into sections of 30 to 40 animals, each group with a man or two to urge them on. While we urged our carrier to stay close by, he would often go faster than our plodding horses. We sometimes would see his umbrella in the midst of tossing horns, knowing that a yak can be very excitable if its load slips. In spite of our warnings our carrier was imperturbable, for he didn't feel he was taking any risks that he couldn't handle. One day we had a river crossing too deep for him to make on foot. "I'll have to ride across with her" he said. "Take your daughter out of the basket," he instructed us." Now I need your horse," he told me. When I handed Marion up to him, he put her into the big, loose fold of his sheepskin robe. Betty had taken off her little pink hat lest it fall in the water. I could see her hair blowing in the breeze. Betty rode her horse across, while he followed on my horse. Marion just enjoyed her thumb during the crossing, but I noted that the poor fellow was perspiring, his face screwed up with the tension of the crossing. He certainly was glad to hand Marion over to Betty. Riding back, he asked me to mount. Then he scrambled on behind me. It wasn't nearly as scary as watching that first trip had been, for if we got a bit wet, so what? The next day we came to another good-sized river, and the carrier didn't like the idea of carrying Marion across by himself. This time he arranged with one of the caravan men, who had a very strong horse, to carry Marion, tucked in his robe, through the river. It made me realize how very responsible for Marion's safety the carrier felt. He obviously didn't want anything dangerous to happen to her.

At the close of a day's march, which could be as early as eleven o'clock in the morning, I would quickly get our small light-weight tent up. It was handy, for we carried it strapped behind Betty's saddle. It provided a place where Marion could stretch and play because it had a waterproof floor and netting at the opening to shield her from flying insects.

*I would quickly get our small
light-weight tent up.*

One such day after we had had some rest, I suggested to Betty that we go for a short walk. Lozongdrema could keep a watchful eye on Marion for us. The two of us went over the brow of a grassy ridge and were surprised to see several of the caravan men grouped around a yak, which was lying on the ground. Curious as to what was going on, we walked over. The men looked a bit surprised and sheepish, but one of them said, "Too bad! This yak has just died." Some of the men snickered, and we took a good look. The beast had indeed died but not from natural causes. Its legs were tied together as was its muzzle, and grass was stuffed up its nostrils. We walked on "I've heard of this," I told Betty. "They suffocate an animal but claim that it died by itself a little later. That way they don't feel guilty about killing a living creature. I'm sure that we will all have meat for supper tonight."

Indeed, we bought some yak meat that night, enough for many more nights on the trip. The extra meat was simply slung up on loads to dry out in the sun and wind. A man would take out his knife and slice off a hunk to chew on as he walked along behind the yak. If birds came down and landed on the meat, one of the men would take expert aim at them with a stone and off they would flap.

During World War II a motor road had been built as far as Ganzi, but like the road up to Kangding, it had fallen into disrepair. At times we followed it, but more often we took the old shortcut trails. Some of these tracks were fit only for a mountain goat. One particularly long march we were forced into a slow motion walk behind the yak, up and down the steep slopes of the barren hills. The sun was blazing down on us while we gazed longingly at the rushing river in the valley and the white ribbon of the unused motor road close to the water's edge far below us. It wound through inviting pastures and slim green evergreens. That was not for us. We crept on for eleven hours, and, reaching a camp spot, we found no water nearby. By the time we did have hot tea, fixed food and rolled in for the night, we just beat the darkness. After days like this Betty would slip off the horse and stand, grasping the saddle for a while before venturing to take a step because she was so stiff. Another day stood out for us because of the high wind we had to endure. It howled and whistled past our ears, sending grit and dust into our mouth and eyes. Betty told me afterwards, "I felt that if the wind would stop I could bear it, and the wind didn't stop. So I found I could bear it anyway!"

We knew summer travel to be more pleasant, and many

days we thoroughly enjoyed the grasslands with their summer flowers — red, yellow, and blue. When we dropped down into the valley near Daowu, we began to pass home-steads and fields ready for harvest. Our dog, White Bear, was getting acclimated once again to life on the road and was having a wonderful time. When we got a room in an old castle near the town, we were besieged by curious people. Suddenly White Bear, who had been lying under a table, lunged out at them with a threatening growl. That was the end of the throng of bystanders for a while. We were by ourselves after that until some patients came, a familiar scene to our dog, and he left them alone.

Long before, a Protestant missionary had tried to live in this town and had been chased out. Catholic priests had suffered here but had managed to keep a work going. I went around to visit Father Doublet, the resident priest, as a matter of courtesy and found him delighted to meet a rare foreign visitor. He was most interested that we planned to start a work in Ganzi. "Yes," he said, "I heard from the Tibetans that some foreign women just passed through our valley. That's very unusual. We used to have the stocky Australian from the Protestant mission come through here and more recently the tall American. But women, no! And now you bring one more woman, your wife! Do give her my greeting and tell her that I admire her courage in coming to this region with a baby daughter!"

He told me how the power of the lamaseries along this road had been very strong. "Years ago no foreigner, even a Chinese, would have been allowed to live in Ganzi," he said, puffing on his pipe. "But the monasteries fell to fighting among themselves, and when they had weakened each other, the Chinese troops came in and defeated them. The princely castles have been destroyed in Ganzi, and you may be permitted to stay in the town. You say that you will do medical work. That should help a lot. I have a Chinese dispenser of medicine here, who is much in demand by the local people."

When I returned to our third-floor room in the former castle, Betty was tending to some patients who needed treatment. Dongwa was subdued and no problem. He had become used to the medical routine back in Batang.

Later as we traveled again, we camped one day on a grassy island in a stream. As I was putting up our tent, a Tibetan walked up leading a horse which bore a girl. He looked weary but glad to see us. "I heard the foreign doctor was on the road, but I had to take two days to catch up with you," he said. "My daughter is in great pain because of sores on her legs. Please, will you help her?" He was addressing me, but I explained my wife was the "doctor" in question. He helped his daughter off the horse while Betty went for her medical kit. When she examined her patient, she found the ulcers in a dreadful state. They were deep, and it would take more than a few dressings to heal them. Betty tried explaining this, but the girl's father just grinned. "Yes, yes!" he said. Betty finally told him, "What you really need to do is to come to Ganzi with your daughter and stay for a while. Unless we can treat her for some weeks, she won't heal."

"Oh, yes, I'll bring her," he said. "It will take a few days for us to make ready." He went over to his horse and brought back a sack with some potatoes in it. These he deposited at Betty's feet. He placed the palms of his hands together in a respectful salute to her, saying, "Thank you", over and over. This poor but dignified farmer was named Dawa and his daughter was called Sonam. After we shared some tea and food with them they said goodbye and left. "I hope they come to see us in Ganzi," Betty said. "I don't think those sores will heal with the small amount of medicine I gave Dawa."

One evening later on this trip I noticed the men camped next to us counting and recounting their yak. I went over. "We are one short," they said, "and we'll have to go and look for it.

It is too late now, so we'll have to do it in the morning."

The next morning we did not break camp, and a search party went after the missing animal. Several hours later they returned, driving the missing yak in front of them. From the flopping and bouncing of the boxes on either side, we could tell they were empty. Someone had spotted the lone animal and ransacked its loads. They contained some of Hester's medicines as well as personal possessions. During the remainder of the trip the men were particularly careful about our loads, and the broken boxes which we took along were a constant reminder to them of that loss. I was pleasantly surprised by the honorable way in which they agreed to a settlement when we arrived in Ganzi, paying Hester fifteen bundles or sixty bricks of tea without any argument. One of the older men interceded for the young man who had owned the wayward yak, and we could tell their relief at her accepting this as compensation.

Marion caught a cold in one farmhouse where we had a drafty room. We were up a good bit at night, rocking her to sleep. We wouldn't have had a room if Lozongdrema hadn't rushed in and found it. She assured the lady of the house that we must have a room to ourselves, thanked her for the use of it before she had even consented, and whispered to Betty, "Stay in here. She might lock the door if you go out." So Betty took possession of a bed platform and sat right there as a woman swept and raised the choking dust in the room.

In spite of these efforts Marion's cough continued and grew worse. Our last night on the road in our tent I took her into my double-down sleeping bag and breathed on her before she stopped coughing. Thus, it was a great relief the next day when we rounded a curve and came out on the magnificent Ganzi plain. At 11,750 feet altitude it still can be cultivated. What captures the eye most is the range of high snow peaks stretching along the south side of the valley. We had a sense of immensity as we had at Litang, but the scene was far fairer. Cultivated fields ready for harvest, groves of trees, and a broad river!

The road goes straight as an arrow from one end of the valley to the other, a three hour march for us. Here and there we saw the roofs of small temples, and then, built against a commanding hillside, there was the Ganzi monastery with its golden roof glittering in the sunlight.

Ganzi town and lamasery.

This had been the capital of the five Hor states – the Kangsar, Beri, Driwo, Drango, and Mazur princedoms– through which we had been passing for the last few days. The walls of the Gelupa monastery were red and white. The princely palaces, partly in ruins, were whitewashed. More than three thousand monks could be housed up in the monastery. Only as we drew close to the town could we begin to make out the squalid, cluttered houses below the confines of the golden-roofed monastery. "I wonder where our ladies are staying," I said to Betty. Lozongdrema had already inquired of a passerby, and she told us that she learned that they were living down toward the river. We headed that way and rounded a bluff, coming on a cluster of new construction, Chinese style, two-story houses. And there were the ladies, standing in Tibetan gowns in a doorway, having spotted our caravan from far off. We gladly dismounted, and they welcomed us into the house.

"How did you ever find a place as nice as this?" we asked.

"You like it?" they responded. "We have been waiting for you to come before telling the landlord – Mr. Ma next door – that we would take it. But it's so much better than the crowded little place we first had up in the town.

"On arrival we rode up to the home of the Kangsa princess, but a surly monk refused us entrance to her palace. Even when we presented a letter for her! Well, a Chinese Christian came along and found a place where we could stay. The next day we hunted further and discovered this brand new place was vacant, spoke for it, and moved in. We really like it."

"We couldn't ask for more," Betty replied, "unless it would be for a cup of tea, our style!"

"Here it comes," said Edie, bringing in a tea tray. We luxuriated in a place of our own after almost a month on the road. It couldn't have come too soon as far as Marion and her cold was concerned. Perfect timing and beautifully arranged. This was hardly the bleak picture we had had described to us in Kangding. I looked out the windows in various directions. "We're surrounded by temples on every side," I said, "four of them. I wonder what the monks and common people of Ganzi are saying about us. And what they'll be saying a few months from now when our clinic has been operating."

CHAPTER 15

THE CLINIC OPENS

"Mr. Wang, who found a place for us that first night, told us that seven years ago even Chinese could not live in Ganzi, let alone foreigners like us," Hester told us.

"That's what we heard from the French priest in Daowu." I replied. "I remember Geoff asking us in Kangding, 'What if you aren't allowed to stay in Ganzi? What are your plans?'"

"Yes, suppose we had allowed ourselves to be scared off coming by outdated information," Edie said. "Just think what we would have missed! There is a sense of welcome spaciousness about this valley."

"And the freedom to call me, 'Old lady! Old lady!' when we came into town," laughed Hester. "Edie and Margaret have dark braids, and they don't stand out to the Tibetans like I do with my fluffy, light hair. But I must admit that those who called me old did so in a friendly way."

"And how did your trip go?" I asked. They had enjoyed it except for some threatening moments. Like when eight armed men rode by their caravan, possibly bandits looking them over. Or when they passed five mounds, and the muleteers announced, "These are the graves of our companions, killed by robbers on our last trip." And one evening Mako had collected all the pot lids and empty cans he could find, stringing them together around their tent. "This will give you an alarm," he told the ladies, "I overheard some of the caravan men talking about how many things you have and how easy it would be to steal some of them from under the flaps of the tent."

Mako must have been under some strain, feeling responsible for the party and their safety. He made a point of telling the caravan men that these foreigners were "under the protection of the Chinese government" and that if anything happened to them that the government would retaliate severely. If any of them did entertain ideas of robbing the ladies, they must have decided to forget about it, for nothing was stolen.

"The fellow in charge of our horses was very unsatisfactory," Edie told us. "His name was Loshi, and he tried to give us poor saddles and poor horses. Mako had such a wretched animal that as we arrived, it collapsed just outside of town, and it died on the spot!"

"Well, we seem to get through some tight spots," I remarked. "But at least we get through. And then we find an ideal house like this all prepared and waiting for us."

New Town at Ganzi, where we were located, was an ambitious construction project which resulted in about 20 houses being partially built on the road leading down to the Yalung River and on to Lhasa. Most of them were empty because the expected Chinese settlers had failed to come and fill them. The building closest to Ganzi was whitewashed, and its woodwork painted in bright colors. It was a duplex, with Mr. Ma, a Moslem merchant, on one side, and our party on the other. Each side had three roomy sections, with a double door in the center section, and windows at the front of the sections on the right and left. Each of the downstairs windows was protected by a half circle of wooden stakes, filled with rocks from the ground up to the level of the window. These stakes were enclosed at the top as security against thieves or marauders. No one would break through these defenses very easily.

The central hall downstairs would serve as a waiting room and the right section would be adequate for the dispensary. The other side we could use for storage and kitchen. When we got extra partitions upstairs, we had six rooms up there and a flat clay roof top at the back. Betty, drying her hair in the sun on that "porch", had icicles form in her hair. It was a reminder that we were at around 11,750 feet altitude, and we could understand why the peaks of Snowy Long Pass Mountain across the valley never lost their snow. At this altitude it was still possible to have some cultivation, but the only trees were in the protected gardens belonging to the monastery. One of these gardens lay in front of our house beside a mill stream. What a restful, pleasant place to be! The river then went surging down through the mountains and was the same "Fish River" to the south that we had crossed by raft at Yajiang en route to and from Batang.

Getting the clinic open downstairs was top priority because patients came daily for help. "I had a shoulder dislocation to handle on our trip up," Hester told us. "I had never done it before, and I was so glad that when I applied pressure, the bone slipped into place. I'll be glad to get my medical books out and have them available for the next tough case I tackle."

Mr. Ma, the landlord, left a large cupboard and a grain bin on our ground floor, the type which would have been used in a shop to display goods or hold stock. The bin had a cover, so Hester chose it to be her examination tale, and the cupboard held a good supply of medicine. As we unpacked boxes we converted them into a desk, seats, and extra tables. Hester as our only registered nurse was in charge and handled the bulk of medical cases. She would be vying with local practitioners and their use of Chinese or Tibetan herbal remedies. Edie, who was a practical nurse, had the responsibility for dentistry. She could occasionally fit reading glasses for the nearsighted, using a collection of secondhand glasses she had brought with her.

Betty, who had the same practical nurse training as Edie, would make some house visits, and sometimes I would accompany Mako on trips out of town. But most mornings activities centered at the dispensary. Mako knew that he wouldn't get people to stand in line. The best he could do was to register people, give them a number, and let them mill around in the entry hall.

One day Dawa and his daughter, Sonam, whom Betty had treated on our trip, showed up, greeting us like old friends. Hester examined Sonam's leg and saw signs of healing, but she said to her, "It's good you came when you did. We're going to keep you here and help you until your legs are completely well."

Sonam being treated by Hester.

The two of them came faithfully to the clinic for dressings

with the result that Sonam's ulcers cleared up completely. Dawa said apologetically, "How can I pay you for healing my daughter? I am a poor man, and I've used up all that I brought with me."

"You don't owe us anything," Hester told him, for we never charged those unable to pay. He wasn't satisfied with that. "I want to pay you back," he declared "If you ever have need of my services, call for me from my village, and I will come." Later we were to take him up on his word.

Betty and I made our first house call to a patient up in Ganzi. Betty found a man with a growth in his abdomen and complications with dropsy. She gave him some medicine that would ease his pain, but that was all she could do for this Tibetan. He died shortly after that, and we heard that his body was thrown in the river. That was one method of disposal, another being "sky burial". This was conducted on the ridge right behind the dispensary where bodies were cut to bits and left exposed for vultures to consume. We often had some of these ugly birds lumbering calmly around on the road in front of the dispensary.

Our next errand of mercy together was when a priest rode up, leading two other riding animals. He was asking for a home visit to an elderly nun, sister of the abbot of the Ganzi monastery. Nurse Hester wasn't free to go, so we two made the exploratory visit to get the details for her. I rode on a large, black mule while Betty had a small chestnut pony. Even with a Tibetan gown on, she managed to mount with grace. We rode up past the town and monastery and then passed a high lama with a golden platter hat, riding in the other direction. We noted that the priest who was accompanying us dismounted and stood at attention as this lama of higher rank came by.

Our destination was a small hillside temple overlooking a cluster of farmhouses. On reaching the lower courtyard of the temple, we had to give wide berth to the watchdog, which lunged as far as his chain would allow in our direction. As we mounted several flights of stairs toward the upper stories of this retreat house we passed several stuffed horses, cows and dogs hanging like dusty balloons from the ceilings. They were covered with dust, so they had been in their places of honor for quite some time.

At the top floor we came to a guest chamber with refreshments awaiting us: thick sour cream, hardboiled eggs, bread, butter and tea. The servants urged us to rest and eat and then disappeared once we began to sample the food. The servants finally returned and ushered us to the old nun's bedchamber. It was ornately decorated as a prayer chapel. The woman described her symptoms which Betty diagnosed as a chronic complaint she could handle. That is always a great satisfaction for all parties concerned. This old lady was well pleased with the results in her case. She continued to send to the clinic for more of the wonderful foreign medicine, always sending gifts of food to express her gratitude.

One day a group of riders on richly decked-out horses came to the clinic. This was a wealthy landowner and his retainers, coming for help because his only son had been shot. Hester and Edie went out for a two-day visit to the large country house where the young man lay, fighting for his life. The story that unfolded was not a pleasant one. This son had been caught in the act of adultery with a woman whose enraged husband had shot him. The father in turn sent out his men to hunt down the husband and kill him. "Yes," said one of the men riding along beside the two ladies, "We did it quickly. We killed him for what he did to the young master."

The family home was a well-constructed manor, freshly painted and clean. Its apartments were richly furnished by Tibetan standards. The patient lay in pain on a sleeping platform. Though Hester explored the wound she was unable to locate the bullet. The men clustered around her, expecting her to extract it. She shook her head as she explained that the bullet had penetrated so far that it would take surgery to get it out. Forceps wouldn't do it. And surgery was something she could not do. She was a nurse, not a doctor. The family felt disappointment, of course, but still treated her with the utmost courtesy. Hester did what she could to ease the young man's discomfort. Then they returned home. In the next few days several of us had occasion to make the trip out to take medicines and help the patient, who was failing rapidly.

When Betty and I came out on a visit, his legs were swelling. This was a sign that the end was near. The family in desperation had called in a troop of monks to read the Buddhist canon of scripture at the usual breakneck speed and to chant their prayers. They draped the patient with extra ribbons and charms around his neck. I noticed a yak down in the courtyard, also decorated with ribbons. I asked a monk, "Why is that yak wearing ribbons?"

"He has been bought and offered to the spirits," he answered, "so that if the spirits spare the young man's life, this yak in return will be guaranteed his life and no work to do for the rest of its days."

When the nobleman's son finally died, the family had a postmortem examination. That is, when the body was cut up for "sky burial", the pieces to be fed to the birds, they found the bullet was indeed far out of reach. Thus, Hester was vindicated, and the family accepted the inevitable outcome. As we reflected over this emergency where both lamas and we were called in to help, at least our nurses gave witness as being careful and compassionate. We were dealing with a powerful man, the father, seeking to appease the unseen world by his influence and purse, meanwhile taking any possible advantage we might give.

We gradually began to learn more of the dynamics of Tibetan society. For example, practically no one visited our dispensary without inquiring first of a priest whether or not he gave permission to enter our doors. Thus, if a patient benefited from our medicine, the priest would take the credit for sending the patient to us. On the other hand, if the sick were forbidden to come, and they died, that was their karma or fate. Hester and Edie had the distress of knowing of desperately ill people who were stopped from coming to the dispensary for help, some of them even after having begun to improve under treatment. This was generally due to priestly interference.

"The lama knows," was a common refrain – for a person's priest was the final authority in all major decisions and many minor ones. We sought to understand the workings of the monastic system. The main monastery dominated the town of Ganzi, but how did it operate? As an institution it was somewhat fragmented into a number of separate "houses". Some of these were wealthy and prestigious, others poor. Each monk represented his own family and received support from them, usually gifts of grain, tea, butter, cloth and salt. If he was a shrewd trader, he could increase his capital. The family or clan would also need to give a young nephew to monastic life in order to provide someone to inherit the monk uncle's holdings. In the absence of a family member in the priesthood, at a monk's death his property would go to the monastery. Some families were too poor to endow their own family priest in the monastery. In that case a young monk would practically be a servant to some other priest. The three single ladies met and began to feed one skinny little monk who had been sold by his mother into service in the monastery. He was a lively little fellow with winning ways. They finally bought his freedom from his master and gave him back to his mother. Samuel, as they named him, came to them daily for nourishing meals. The effect of this was dramatic, and Samuel began to emerge as a very active, growing boy.

We did not long delay the wedding of Lozongdrema and

Mako. We arranged with our neighbor, Mr. Ma, for the use of a small building in the back garden where the couple would be able to live. As a Muslim, he would not attend the wedding feast we planned. We were having it catered, and some of the dishes would contain pork. We secured a number of household items as gifts for the couple, including the usual embroidered quilts which a bride would prize. We had the ceremony in the upstairs living room above the dispensary. Lozongdrema was practically speechless with embarrassment, but we got through the vows. Then our small group sat down together for the wedding feast.

Betty and I wanted to move into the town of Ganzi, right below the lamasery ten minutes away, even though it didn't seem likely that we could find a suitable apartment there. However, once the word got out, it was not long before we had a visit from two Tibetans who told us they would be glad to have us share a part of their compound. Betty and I gladly followed them through the narrow, twisty lanes, between walls covered with drying cow patties. We entered a nondescript courtyard with a tethered donkey but no watchdog. To the side of the main door was an additional wing. A family occupied the ground floor of the wing but the second floor was vacant. We followed the owners up a rickety staircase without a railing and found ourselves standing on an earthen porch. "Look," said one of the men, "you can use the corner room in the main house which opens out on this porch. And you have two rooms here, one of which is a kitchen." We were favorably impressed by the room in the main house with its wooden floor and colorful wall decorations. The two rooms in the wing extension had whitewashed walls though their rafters were a glistening, greasy black from much smoke. Our kitchen had a hole in the earthen floor, which brought us the kitchen smoke from the family down below. Lastly, the bathroom facilities could be described as simple and well ventilated. We didn't argue about some of the obvious disadvantages to this apartment but quickly closed the deal.

Afterwards we discovered why our Tibetan landlord was so eager to have us. The apartment we had rented had been the Chinese Nationalist party office, recently vacated. The party signboard was still stored over in a corner. As these Tibetans didn't want more Chinese officials quartered in their compound, they hustled to offer us the rooms before some other Chinese bureau or department insisted on having them. We may have offended the Chinese officials in town, but we hoped that our medical help would mollify them.

Recently we had fallen under suspicion. The first we knew about it was when Mako came back from the police station. The chief was inquiring of him if we were transmitting radio messages. The chief had a report that observers had noted that we had strung up aerials and had heard us tapping out messages. Mako was puzzled by these accusations, but he finally figured out that what they were talking about were our clotheslines and typewriters. He explained what we actually had, and we heard no more on that subject. This was typical of the rumors that circulated in the uneasy political climate. The existing Chinese government was disintegrating nationwide.

Soon after the American election of 1948, the results arrived in Ganzi. Local Chinese officials revealed their discouragement to me, saying "It's hopeless for China now because the new government in America will not provide enough aid for us to use against the Communists. We're finished!" If that was the attitude even here, I knew the days of the Chiang Kai-shek government were numbered.

One place where we found a warm welcome was at the post office, for the postmaster was interested in getting to know us. He had just arrived, and he confided in me, "When I heard that some foreigners were moving to Ganzi, I chose the position here." He volunteered a room in the post office

178

for us to hold Sunday services. In addition, his assistant, also newly arrived, was a young Christian, Lo, from the church in Kangding. We were off to a flying start. Lo plunged into Tibetan studies in his spare time, a rare occupation for a Chinese official. He said that he wanted to share his faith with Tibetans just as he had seen John Ding doing in Kangding.

Margaret began Bible classes for women at the post office, including the postmaster's wife and Lo's young wife among the women who gathered. It was something of a nursery as well. Betty often took little Marion along with her, and she played happily with the other children. The study group grew in numbers and infectious laughter. Mostly young mothers, they had a lot in common.

We were far removed from the outside world and its problems. Betty's daily life had more to do with how to cope with the smoke billowing up from downstairs. Our own fire would build up a layer of haze in the kitchen and dining room. As Betty supervised the boiling of baby dishes over our stove, her eyes would sting. Stirring Marion's cereal, she would dab at them to no avail. "My hands are either dirty or dry as a bone from this constant washing," she remarked with a wry smile. The water we used was carried in from a nearby stream. The woman carrier had an amazing sense of balance as she teetered up our steps without spilling a drop.

At harvest time, we could hear the cheery songs of the harvesters and then the threshing crews on surrounding rooftops. Some threshing took place down in our courtyard. All over town straw was being stacked for winter feed. The long horns blown at the monastery now had the competition of harvest songs. I could imagine myself back in Babylon or Thebes, privy to some ancient rites. While we had lived in Batang, we were some distance from the temples. Here we were enfolded by them. Up the hillside behind us about a hundred yards were tier upon tier of whitewashed monastery buildings looming over us. They were topped by the glare of gleaming gold leaf roofs, certainly evidence of a sturdy status quo.

The harvesters

An occasional Chinese in this region seemed to be reaching out to us. A school teacher wrote to me from Jyekundo, two hundred miles to the northwest, asking me to send him some Christian literature. After I mailed him some, he wrote back to me from his lonely post, "Both your letter and books have been received. What a valuable gift for me, just as a desert traveler found his fount, so I have made up my mind that from now on I should put myself in practice according to the Bible and your precious telling. I can believe that God would strengthen and keep me forever, if I could read the Bible, and pray to the Lord Jesus every time and everywhere."

I also heard from the telegraph operator in Batang, whom I had befriended earlier in the year. He told me, "I have read the Gospel and Way of Salvation booklet over and over again, and I always go to church now. I wrote the words of my intent to serve God and sent this to Pastor Lee. After this I will respect Christ and obey what he says and do what he asks." It was clear to me that we were meeting a heart need of some Chinese and some Tibetans.

Within two weeks of our arrival in Ganzi we had had three Tibetans come forward and tell us of their previous acquaintance with Christians, one of them having come from Amdo far in the north and another from India, where he had been in a church boarding school. Jimba from Amdo was working for Mr. Ma, our landlord. He would take trade goods around the surrounding hamlets and sell them for his master. Jimba had remembered a number of Christian songs, and he had some understanding of their meaning to him personally. When both he and Drashi, the older woman who had come with us from Kangding, professed their faith I baptized them. The other acquaintance who mentioned having some knowledge of Christianity from visits to Kangding was friendly but kept his distance on spiritual matters.

Then we faced a crisis, for an epidemic of a strange throat infection spread among children of the town. Our nurses were busy, going from home to home as they were called, often too late to be of help. Moreover, desperate parents would use Chinese and Tibetan medicines as well. The nurses never did discover what the virus was, but it was virulent, attacking small children and wasting them in twenty-four hours. The day we learned that the postmaster's family had lost their little daughter to this disease was rainy and dark. I remember so well sitting with Betty at our small square table in the semi-darkness. Our delightful Tibetan adventure had taken a somber turn.

At suppertime, Betty lit a candle, for we had to close the door and wooden window blind. She looked at me and said, "Marion played with Mei-hua just two days ago. She's probably been exposed." Mei-hua was the postmaster's daughter.

"We had better pray," I suggested.

"I can't pray," she replied. That is the only time I have ever heard her say that, and I was thunderstruck. We sat there more or less in silence, eating our tsamba and drinking butter tea. Marion was asleep in her crib in the bedroom, a crib which I had made out of wood from the organ crate. After about an hour Betty suddenly spoke up and said "I can pray. I feel as though a black cloud has rolled away. Somehow I feel different. I have faith that God will protect Marion." So we prayed for her safety. Betty wrote a letter to her mother in Toronto, Canada that same day, describing her experience of confusion followed by a sense of great peace. Marion never caught the virus, and we were so thankful. But the extraordinary thing we learned came in her mother's reply. She wrote, "I read your air form out to Mrs. McLulich. She prays regularly for you and always wants me to share any news. When she heard how you couldn't pray, Betty, she looked excited. She asked me to figure out what time it was here in Toronto when you heard about the death of that child and couldn't pray. The same time Mrs. McLulich awoke out of a sound sleep. She had a strong feeling that you were in trouble. She got up and prayed for you until she had the assurance that you were all right. Then she went back to bed, and now we know why that happened to her. God reached around the world and found someone to help you just when you needed it."

That incident reminded us of what Gladys Schwake had told us about her mother and a friend who were impressed to pray for her just when she was at a dangerous spot on a narrow ledge above a river. With God at work for us, we were not as isolated as it would seem. We were not alone, nor were new believers even in times of loss.

Chinese dollar currency was no longer of use to anybody in Ganzi. We had to buy a $200,000 stamp to send a foreign air letter, and how long could the post office keep turning out new and higher denomination stamps? Shipments of goods from down country could be erratic. In an emergency I recall going one day to the local market by the mill stream and gaining a small amount by selling empty bottles and tins to eager Tibetans. The smaller the bottle, the better, for they were always looking for snuff bottles. They didn't use opium or cigarettes, but they did have a fondness for snuff.

One day Edie Seager was looking for some tinned goods in a storeroom when she noticed that a tin of jam had been punctured. Surprised, she investigated further and discovered that tin after tin had been partially opened. She called Hester and Margaret and together they checked their whole inventory only to find that some tins were missing. This was a mystery because the storeroom was kept locked. Then they noticed that near the ceiling there was a gap in the wall sufficient for a person to squeeze through from Mr. Ma's house. Mr. Ma quickly investigated and found his wife had some of the tins. She had climbed up and over in order to satisfy her curiosity regarding what treasures the foreigners kept in that room. Poor woman, she got a severe beating from her husband. He always spoke of her to us with contempt as "my thing." He was a male chauvinist of the worst sort, contemptuous of his daughter and idolizing of his son. This was in such contrast to the trust and responsibility Tibetan women bore.

We assessed our losses and made haste to eat some of the fruit and other opened food. It was quite a blow to us because we knew these sorts of tinned goods were disappearing from the Chengdu markets with the departure of American military advisors from China. We would have preferred to dole these treats out on special occasions.

CHAPTER 16

MEDICS ON CALL

❖

Illness is a great leveler, and we found that out when the princess, the Kangsa Bemo, had a child with a bad cold. She sent an urgent message requesting someone from the clinic to come to the palace, a large mansion. The Ganzi valley had been divided from time immemorial between the Kangsa tribe and the Mazur tribe. The farmers on the valley floor provided food and services to the head of their tribe on a rotation basis. The Mazur princely family had been wiped out by war, but the Kangsa family still received their due in time and tribute from their people. Kangsa Bemo had married a Lhasan noble as her consort, but she was the native ruler. That she had borne several sons and daughters to replenish her family line made her very popular.

The reputation of our clinic nurses was spreading widely, and we began to get calls from a distance. The ladies would have enjoyed responding to some of these invitations, but it didn't seem practical to have them leave Ganzi unattended and to endure the hard travel involved. For example, two young Tibetans, extremely well-dressed from their fur hats to their bright-colored boots, rode up one day and insisted on an immediate audience with Nurse Hester. "We came from the prince of Drango," they announced. "The old prince is suffering, and we are afraid he will die. Please come immediately, and see if you can help him. We have brought along extra horses for you and a companion to ride."

Knowing that this would involve an especially fast trip of sixty miles in two days, Hester asked Mako and me to go and at least bring back a report on the man's condition. She was not too hopeful, considering the patient's age, but she prepared medicines and instructions for us.

We left at a gallop with the two men, Sonam and Tsepel. All went well until Tsepel's horse stumbled and sent him flying. He picked himself up, brushed himself off, examined his horse, and remounted without comment. Then he started off at the same speed again. We took less than 24 hours, spending the night in the five-story castle at Driwo. The open windows and a hearty wind kept me burrowed in my sleeping bag, and still I was cold in our third-floor room. It was the best ventilated Tibetan building I could remember!

On arrival at the Drango Castle we were not rushed to the bedside of the patient. Rather we were given a chance to rest. Servants plied us with delicious food and butter tea. They gave us tea from an ornate teapot beside us on a brazier. We learned that the old prince had retreated to the top floor of the palace in order to "escape the noise" a troop of lamas were making in the building. We heard their sonorous tones starting low and steadily rising. It was enough of a hubbub to bother us, let alone a sick man.

Mako and I talked over how we would proceed. Basically the case was his responsibility, not mine. Lacking medical training, I wouldn't remove a splinter very well. My presence with him was meant to be a backup and to indicate our respect for the prince. Of course, I received deference as a foreigner, but I wasn't a doctor. My "second opinion" was just for Mako in case he wondered if he was exceeding Hester's instructions.

As we climbed up the notched pole to the roof, I wondered how the prince got there, probably on a man's back. He was huddled under a mound of covers in a sheltered alcove. "He looks like he needs a hot water bottle," I suggested to Mako. We began asking questions of the old man and of his retainers. We ended up with so many symptoms that I murmured to Mako that we should retreat to our room downstairs and decide what to do about a diagnosis. "Let's give him something – an aspirin, a tablet of bicarb," Mako answered. That was inspired, and a green aspirin brought a smile to the prince's face. For two days Mako gave him some injections that Hester had suggested. This procedure was always most impressive to a patient and any bystanders. You really hadn't done much for a client if you didn't give a shot. Mako was expert at this, so my contribution was looking wise and sympathetic, patting the old man's hand and feeling his brow. We left the man feeling more comfortable and his crisis passed, but we doubted that he had long to live.

Mako and I had enjoyed our spare time at Drango, lots of long walks, opportunities to discuss his hopes and questions, and always food to munch on. Young monks liked to crowd around our alcove, watching with curiosity everything we did. Mako was observant too. "Do you see that pile of clay pellets?" he asked me once.

"Yes, what are they?" I replied.

"They are religious offerings," he told me. "The monks here make them by rolling clay in their fingers. It's a form of gaining merit."

The two of us had ten years' difference in age, for I was 30 while he was 20, but in these surroundings we were drawn together by what we had in common in contrast to the Tibetans around us. While Mako had grown up familiar with their viewpoint and values, he had changed in many respects. And it was on this trip that he confided in me his desire to study for the Christian ministry some day. I reminded him that we foreigners as a group did not employ church workers, and he said that he figured God would provide for him and his family if he was serving God's people. I liked his attitude of faith.

Back in Ganzi our study of the surrounding region showed us an area like an hourglass on its side from east to west. The Ganzi valley was the first bulge, then a narrow bottleneck, and beyond that the Rombatsa valley on the West side. The town of Ganzi was near this narrow section. I was curious about Rombatsa because that area was within easy reach of where we were living. Just twenty years before, the Rombatsa area had been seized and held by a Tibetan army sent by the Lhasa government of the Dalai Lama. The large Dajen monastery in that valley strongly supported this army, and as a result the monks there suffered when the Chinese eventually regained control. I heard that the Dajen monks still simmered with anger at the Chinese. My opportunity to visit the Rombatsa area came when a young trader's agent named Dawa Dongdru invited me to visit his master's house there. Mako and I agreed to go, and we set out by horse together. Near home we crossed the river, and then followed the south side until we approached the town and monastery of Beri. This was a Sakya monastery called Nyara Gomba. It is situated on a spur looking over the river and painted in sections of red, white and black. There we re-crossed the river and entered the broad Rombatsa plain. The farmhouses looked prosperous, and the castle of the trader we were going to visit was impressive. Dawa Dongdru welcomed us heartily, and introduced us to other members of the trading clan. Then he proudly brought out a radio which he operated with 36 flashlight batteries, and we heard a newscast in Chinese from Guangzhou. None in our group at Ganzi had a radio, so we were way behind on news. What we heard was the fall of Guangzhou to the Communists. That gave me pause, but it still seemed far away down on the China coast.

We stayed two days during which Mako took care of a patient in the large homestead. Then Dawa Dongdru told us a tent festival was in process. Would we like to move to the campgrounds below Dajen Gomba? Yes indeed! Many from the castle had already gone there. This was too good to miss, a memorable sight – a field covered with the white cloth tents used for such occasions. These tents had black appliquéd designs on them which heightened their beauty. Dawa took us to one of the tents belonging to his trading firm, and we were soon aware of a lot of curious youngsters staring at us under the edges of the tent flaps.

The word spread, and Mako and I were asked to come to the large main tent of the abbot of the Dajen Gomba, the local monastery. The object of the call was a little boy, the abbot's nephew, who lay pale and wasted under a blanket. He looked very much like a victim of tuberculosis. We didn't have the specific medicine needed for him, but we could send for it. Meanwhile, we discussed with the abbot what sort of a diet would be helpful to the boy. We warned about his being kept in a smoky environment and urged them to get him out into the sun from time to time.

After surveying this second valley, we estimated that about 25,000 Tibetans lived in the "hourglass" area. "If we ever expanded our medical work, we would open something here," I said to Mako, and he agreed. In fact, he said he would like to be the one to move into Rombatsa valley with Lozongdrema and start a branch clinic. Wonderful dreams, but abruptly on our return to Ganzi Mako had a job offer that was very tempting. A Batang friend of his in the local telegraph office asked him to come and work with him at a salary six times what he was receiving from us. Mako was so conscientious that he had a terrible struggle about this. Lozongdrema, all practicality, couldn't see why he would hesitate for a moment. It was a big step up in the world. Mako on the other hand felt bound by the three-year contract he had signed with us. We didn't hold him to it and told him we would write to Kangding to see if a replacement could be found for his work in the clinic.

The next surprise was a three page telegram from the American Consulate in Chungqing telling us that we should make plans to leave China as soon as possible because the Consulate could not guarantee the safety of its nationals. Pointedly we were informed that if we ignored this warning that the Consulate would take no further responsibility for us. In fact, it would soon close.

Hester, Margaret, little Marion and I were Americans. Betty and Edie were Canadians. The British Consulate was evidently not ready to issue a warning, but we debated what we should do. "I'm still taking care of the soldier with the gunshot wound," said Hester. "He's a lot better and out of danger, but really I'm needed here." This soldier had been shot on the dangerous Daowu pass. When he arrived back in Ganzi, Hester had been called on to amputate his arm. Instead she saved it, much to the man's joy and that of his Tibetan wife.

"I think Betty and I should go down with Marion to Kangding before the winter weather sets in," I said. "We can't get all the facts we need from here. The major question is whether the postal service and the banks are going to continue or close up shop. Also, we need to replenish our medical stocks and our reserves of brick tea and silver dollars if we're going to hang on up here or move into inner Tibet. We might locate some credit links with Kalimpong in India."

190

Our team discusses whether to go or to stay.

The three ladies agreed with us that it could be dangerous for Marion if we were forced to travel with her in the
depth of winter. I advised them to prepare to leave if necessary, saying "I can't tell what we'll find out in Kangding. I
may have to ask you to follow us, so you might be thinking
about what you would take and what you would leave
behind in an emergency."

Betty began to think how Marion would travel. "She's
too big to travel all day in a basket," she said, "and I don't

have that much confidence in your horsemanship, David, to want you to carry her on your horse."

"What about sending for Dawa, the man who brought his daughter here for medicine?" I suggested. "We got to know him, and he offered to help us if we needed him."

Betty was pleased with the idea, and we sent a message to his village. He came promptly and with a happy grin on his face. We talked with a caravan leader and asked him if he could leave on a Thursday. He seemed reluctant but finally agreed to go on that day. Later a Tibetan friend seemed surprised that we should be leaving on that particular date. "It's an unlucky day," he assured us. "I don't believe there will be a caravan moving anywhere in Tibet on that day."

"But the man promised us," I replied. We began to wonder if he would bring his animals on the day promised. We got ready, and sure enough, he showed up. His men loaded up our pieces while I saddled our riding animals with my Tibetan teacher's help. He was there to see us off. Betty was wearing a bright red wool jacket and had a fox skin tied around her head. She placed Marion in the fur-lined bag she had prepared for the trip. I then lifted our child up to Dawa in his saddle. She would ride in his lap, facing him as shelter from the wind. We helped Dawa with the sash which tied her firmly to him.

Then, with waves to Margaret, Hester, Edie, Mako, Lozongdrema and Drashi as well as to Mr. Ma, we swung out across the stubble in the fields. We were on our way as scheduled, or so we thought! The joke was on us. We only rode for about twenty minutes when we reached a campsite. "This is where we stop for today," the clever Tibetan told us. He had gotten our trade. He had made the start as promised, but he had also managed from a Tibetan point of view to delay our trip until the next morning when he could safely proceed. We had learned once again that if we accommodated ourselves to Tibetan ways we would endure less frustration. At times the part of wisdom was "when in Tibet, accept what the Tibetans do." For two-thirds of our trip we traveled with a large armed group, but one long day we found ourselves all alone.

CHAPTER 17

PRAYER ANSWERED ON A DOORSTEP

T he shadows at the end of that day lengthened on the bare Tibetan hills. A cold wind whipped the fox fur wrapped so jauntily around Betty's head, but she looked anything but jaunty as she leaned forward on the pommel of her western saddle.

"How much farther do you think it is?" she asked me wearily.

I turned in my saddle and called to Dawa, our companion, who was carrying our baby daughter strapped in front of him. She was tucked deeply into her fur-lined bag, facing toward him. "How much farther is it to Gada Gomba?" I asked.

"Just over there," he replied with a mischievous smile, pointing with a wave of his arm toward the brow of the next hill. And he prodded his horse with both his heels as an indication to us that he was as interested as we were in reaching the end of the long day's journey.

For several days we had been attached to a large party, but this morning they had left at four-thirty without calling us. We had scrambled to pack and be off at five-thirty, and in the process Betty had lost her watch. Our loads had gone ahead with the main party, but we three adults and the baby were facing the most dangerous section of the trip without benefit of any visible protection. We had to thread our way through dark pine forests and up over a desolate pass, then over empty tundra, forsaken by nomads and their herds in the winter. On and on and on. I had never felt so exposed to ambush. By this time we had survived three bandit attacks on the road, and that was with many companions. To ride along alone was a "no-no" that I had not imagined our finding ourselves engaged in. We had been told so often that travelers do not travel by themselves and unarmed in unruly Kham Province.

As we approached a pass over an open field, we saw the scattered letters of a rifled mailbag. I picked up one empty envelope addressed to the Catholic priest in Daowu. Poor fellow, I had visited him at his isolated post and knew how much he treasured his few contacts with the outside world.

Dawa seemed unconcerned, but that could be misleading. Perhaps if we recalled that wonderful children's story, "Gone is Gone!" and mentally said goodbye to anything of value we still carried with us, we could act as light-hearted as he. Dawa laughed and joked with little Marion, and she laughed in return, reaching up her little fingers to pull at his straggly moustache. The thermos of hot water we carried with us proved its worth, for we never passed a sign of human habitation during that long day. When we felt hungry, we munched on a few snacks we had in our pockets. To my dismay, when I felt around a deep pocket of my field jacket for a hard-boiled egg, I pulled out a sticky mess of yolk and eggshell. I'd neglected to boil the egg long enough at those high altitudes.

Late in the afternoon and after we had passed ridge after ridge without seeing our destination, Dawa let out a shout of triumph and pointed out a flat-roofed homestead ahead. Here was a promise of shelter for the night. But by the time we reached it, we saw that beyond this the valley opened out on a small plain. Ahead and still at some distance we could see a line of low adobe-type buildings and the higher roofs of the Gada monastery, flanked by tall poplars, a black mass in the fields to the right. We tried to quicken our pace, but our animals were exhausted. We plodded slowly in and found Gada's main street crowded with Chinese soldiers mixed with Tibetans, who were bringing in their animals for the night. Dawa told us a military detachment had come into this small town early enough to preempt most space in the hamlet. We had come too late even though the residents weren't posting "no vacancy" signs. "I can't go any farther," Betty said, sinking down on a wooden step. I gave Marion to her and left to look for a room somewhere. I was refused at every door, and my heart sank. Dawa was also out searching, and he came back, shaking his head. Dusk was falling, and time was running out. Once the doors slammed shut, we would be out in the cold. Marion needed a change and some supper. What could I do?

I would have to try harder. At last down at the end of the street in a disreputable stable I found a man who said we could stay there. But looking through the broken slats, I saw some men lying on boards, smoking opium. Well, that was out of the question, so I went back to Betty.

We had just about reached the limits of what we could take. Here we were finding that the destination we had been looking forward to for so many hours was not the pleasant sanctuary we had hoped for.

I shared what I had discovered with Betty. "The shop-keepers also say they don't have any food. The soldiers have bought it all."

"We're going to have to get in somewhere so that I can take care of Marion and get her to sleep," Betty said.

"That will take a miracle," I replied. "I know that's what we need, so let me pray right now. We know what to do when the odds are against us."

After praying I looked up. The doorway behind Betty had been opened, and an attractive Tibetan woman was standing there watching us. I hadn't seen her before. It was worth a try. "We have a baby," I said. She looked at us with interest. "We need a place to stay. Can you help us?" I added.

She was apologetic as she explained that the rooms she usually rented were already filled. "But we don't need a room, just some space," I pled, "We're used to making do on the floor."

I could see that something I had said had sparked an idea in her mind. She hadn't imagined that foreigners would accept less than basic accommodations. "Well..." she started.

"Yes?" I encouraged.

"I do have an alcove off the hallway," she admitted.

"Do let us see it," I said immediately, and when Betty and I followed her down the narrow hall, we found an empty place to one side about six feet by six. I dropped my saddle bags in the spot to take possession. "This will do," I said, for I could see that Betty was willing to settle for this corner.

Dawa got busy lighting a fire in the kitchen while Betty prepared some food for both of us. When he brought us two bowls of steaming butter tea, our sleeping bags were spread out, and our daughter had had her meal and was fast asleep. It didn't take long before we followed suit, but not before the livestock of the house paraded in the front door and down the passageway beside us and into the back yard.

The lady of the house was a godsend and a wonderful example of Tibetan hospitality at its best. Her name was Tashi, and to our surprise, we found that she was the sister of a woman who had cooked for elderly Mrs. Cunningham down in Kangding. When Tashi found that we were friends of Mrs. Cunningham, she was prepared to do all she could for us. And we certainly needed her help. The town was jammed with travelers, but she saw to it that we had all the food we needed. It took her a week, but she eventually secured the animals we required for the trip on to Kangding. We stayed in our alcove all this time, for none of her rooms emptied out. But Tashi made things pleasant for us simply by her cheerful attitude. I would hear Betty laughing with her in the kitchen and knew that all was well. She appreciated the fact that Betty was not demanding and went out of her way to provide for us, given the limitations of that crowded village. I'm sure that what Betty liked more than anything else about Tashi was that she was instinctively neat and clean, and her house reflected this. Yes, even with the donkey, the cow, and the goats clattering through the house morning and evening. I guess she had them house-trained.

When we finally had transport I said to Betty, "We'll reach Kangding for Christmas after all." A few days later we were back in that border city, glittering with its electric lights, and Christmas once more upon us. It dawned on us that when there were no rooms in the inn at Gada Gomba we had found a humble place for our baby and a caring person. Somehow our experience at Gada helped us understand Bethlehem in a new way. It also showed us another Tibetan woman with a big heart.

Dawa came by to say goodbye before returning to his home halfway up to Ganzi. Marion cooed at him with delight. We thanked him again for his excellent horsemanship and care fording streams. "Don't thank me," he said. "I am so thankful for the way your medicine healed my daughter's leg last year. I was too poor to pay, and you asked for nothing. I am glad I could make this trip for you." We went with him to the gate, Marion in my arms, and waved goodbye.

"Good old Dawa," Betty said, as we went back in, "Marion certainly had more fun with him talking to her than on the trip up to Ganzi when she was in a cradle basket on a man's back."

We had found mail waiting for us in Kangding, including a belated wedding gift of cash for Mako and Lozongdrema from Betty's father. We notified the ladies in Ganzi, knowing that they had enough rupees on hand to advance the gift to them.

Then to our surprise we got a letter from Edie telling us that Mako had lost his job at the telegraph office after two weeks, no explanation having been given to him by the officials there. Evidently his Batang friend had had his choice of Mako overruled. When Edie looked up a crestfallen Mako and handed him one hundred rupees he was quite overcome. "It's a wedding gift from Betty's father," Edie explained. "It's late, but it has come in time to be a Christmas gift for you and Lozongdrema."

"This is like the gift I received last spring in Kangding," he said. At that time he had been tithing his slender income to the Kangding church, and some of his Batang friends were chiding him for not giving substantial gifts to Lozongdrema, his fiancée. In both Kangding and Ganzi now he had had remarkable and unexpected deliverance. "God is trying to remind me to walk by faith, not by sight," he declared.

Mako wrote a letter to the Kangding church telling them his experience of taking the telegraph office position, then losing it, and next the coming of a gift which gave him new hope.

Mako was to be tested further, for one day the couple returned to their rooms to discover that a thief had ransacked the apartment and made off with their most valued possessions. Lozongdrema was inconsolable. She had so little, and now her two best quilts were gone. Some neighbors told Mako that they were sure that an opium addict had robbed them. They knew who it was, and they urged Mako to file a complaint with the police against him.

When Mako refused to do this, Lozongdrema was beside herself with anger, accusing him of being a coward, a poor provider, and anything else she could think of to say. He gazed at her sadly but quietly, and this made her madder. But he was not to be moved. "I know that we've lost these precious things," he said, "but we are supposed to take the spoiling of our goods cheerfully. Maybe you can't, but I can because I believe God will make up to us what we have lost."

Down in Kangding several missionaries had left, but others remained calm. I felt that we needed to have our team together to consider what we should do. I wrote asking them to come as soon as they could. I recommended that Mako be asked to care for the dispensary in New Town. The dispensary would need to close temporarily, but Mako and Lozongdrema could be caretakers of our property. The ladies were able to make arrangements for Mako's salary and handed him a reserve fund of 300 rupees against emergencies. "We trust you," they said, "and you've got a big responsibility for the brothers and sisters here. We wish that we didn't have to leave you like this, but we'll be back as soon as we can."

Now Lozongdrema was four months pregnant. It was hard for the ladies to leave them, so young, so inexperienced, and so vulnerable. Mako had a jut to his jaw that showed his determination to prove himself this time. With no foreigners to lean on he would have to look elsewhere for help. Mako knew the "elsewhere" that could see him through.

CHAPTER 18

WORKING WITH A TIBETAN CHURCH PLANTER

O n our return to the city of Kangding on the Chinese
border, we were touched to realize how well our
friends there had followed the progress of our new work in
Ganzi. They were as concerned as we were that it go forward
and usually the most recent news we had was from Mako.

The letters he wrote detailed some difficulties and
discouragement. One problem none of us had anticipated
was the arrival of an older brother of his on a visit from
Batang. He not only expected Mako to entertain him but
also to lend him money. "Mako doesn't need that kind of
pressure," Betty said, "It puts him in an almost impossible
situation. He can't be inhospitable to his older brother!" So
we prayed about it, and eventually the brother left and made
his way down to Kangding.

While seeking to assess what we should do, we found
housing, got busy with more language study, and followed
the reports of Communist expansion across China. Locally,
church growth went on apace, helped by the arrival of more
Chinese Christian workers with a burden for Tibet. They had

more difficulty with Tibetan pronunciation than we did, and they also found Tibetan food less palatable than we did. But that wasn't going to deter them. We were impressed with the deep commitment of Chinese Christians to reaching the minorities to the West. Twelve of them had come under three Chinese agencies, and they meant business for the Lord.

One of these arrivals was himself a Tibetan from Batang. Wangden was short and stocky. His hair fell across his forehead like mine does. He would scoop it back into place, only to have it fall again. I know just how he felt and why he gave up on it. As we got acquainted, I could see that he was a dynamo underneath a somewhat rough exterior. He could give the impression of being a trifle curt, which really was only the slight impatience of one who found it difficult to bear with fools. But he could break into a smile and capture attention with his flow of speech. I marked him as a natural leader.

Both he and other Chinese coming to the border were strongly independent and didn't want to have any reliance on foreigners or foreign organizations. They were intent on avoiding the "running dogs of the imperialists" label which the Communists had used against Chinese believers.

Wangden wasn't eager to return to Batang, for he felt that he would be something of a prophet without honor in his own country. He talked with two British men who hoped to get into inner Tibet, and they agreed that he could accompany them without obligation and at his own expense. They weren't ready to leave Kangding, however, because they had not completed their financial arrangements to receive credits in Kham from a Tibetan trading house and make payments in India.

I had developed confidence in Wangden, and one day I said to him, "Brother, you've heard of the small band of believers up in Ganzi. Why don't you go up there for a few months and help them? Then you could come back here and go West with the two British brothers, perhaps even into inner Tibet."

He looked at me in surprise. "You mean that you wouldn't mind someone else going up to Ganzi to do Christian work?" he asked, as if we were possessive of the location.

"Of course not, as long as the person has a good character and a sound message," I replied. "And obviously I think you qualify! The church there doesn't belong to us."

"Well, thank you very much," he said, "for frankly I have been getting tired of waiting around here and have been hoping that I could get over Jeddo Pass into my country – real Tibetan country – the open spaces. I feel constrained in this tight valley. I'll have to think and pray about what you have suggested."

Real Tibetan country

I wasn't offering him a job, for we were unwilling to pay church workers. Wangden had no use for foreign paternalism either, so we were on the same wavelength. He saw the problems of young and immature believers at Ganzi as an opportunity he would like to help remedy. One day, having made up his mind, he came to me and said briefly, "I'll go to Ganzi. I know it's the place God want me for the present." I was excited about that.

As he began to make his preparations for the road I had the opportunity to hear his story. "I come from a poor family in Batang," he told me, "and my father died when I was young. A Christian there cared about me and saw that I got enrolled in elementary school. I was so happy. Books fascinated me, and I forged ahead with my reading. Some of the other students complained, but I was so interested in what I was learning. As a result I was top of my class every year I was there.

"That was ten years ago, and I was soon to graduate from the Batang school," he continued. "One afternoon I came out of the school gate and saw a woman teaching a group of children in the street. I knew who she was. Her name was Hannah. She was a Chinese lady, and she had a companion named Mary. They had come to Batang, and she often gathered children together like this. I decided I would have a little fun, so I ducked behind the school wall. From there I began lobbing stones over the wall at her and her audience of children. Then I turned and saw a teacher watching me. I thought he would scold me, but when I said, "It's that Christian woman who teaches in the streets," he smiled and walked away. That man's indifference spurred me to continue my mischief. I pestered the story-telling lady whenever I spotted her out with the children, keeping discreetly out of sight myself but throwing stones. When she gave up and no longer appeared I was very pleased with myself. After all, I shared the views of my teachers that all religion was superstition. To them science was supreme, and in my pursuit of knowledge, I was ready to believe them.

"Because of my academic success I received a scholarship to go down-country for junior middle school. I had a lot of culture shock when I was immersed in Chinese life, but I persevered. I received a scholarship for senior middle school, and my ambition soared. I remember that during my years in high school someone gave me a New Testament. I gladly started reading it, but I found it rather puzzling. One day I came to a verse that struck me as eminently sensible. It was Jesus saying, 'Except a grain of wheat fall in the ground and die, it abides alone; but if it dies, it brings forth much fruit.' I read it over and over, and then slapped the little book down. 'That's me,' I said to myself, 'I'll fall in the ground and die for the sake of Tibetan independence, and because of my death, many other Tibetans will be willing to die for our country.'

"When I completed high school, my grades had been so high that I was given a scholarship to go to university. This university was in a suburb of Chungqing, so I traveled to that city. I recalled that two Tibetans I knew from Batang were studying at a Christian school in Chungqing. When I inquired where the school was, I found that it was almost on the road I would take to my campus. For years I had rarely been with a Tibetan, and I longed to speak my native tongue once more. I decided to try and find them. I would stop at their school and look for them.

"Carrying my bedroll and a few other possessions on my back, I came up to the gate of the school and gave the names of these two students to the gatekeeper. 'Oh yes,' he said, 'They are here. I know them, but all the students are in a meeting just now, in that building over there.' I asked him if I could enter, and when he permitted me, I walked over to the building he had pointed out. Looking in a window, I could see people sitting in a circle, many of them with their heads bowed. Finally I spotted a Tibetan lady I knew. Someone called her out to meet me. She greeted me warmly and asked me to come inside. I was embarrassed but felt

obligated to do what she wanted. I saw people praying with
their eyes shut, but I kept mine open! I flushed when the
Tibetan lady, Naomi, began to pray for me. Then to my
horror others whom I had never met began to pray for this
Wangden who had wandered into their midst. I was taken
aback by their earnestness. I couldn't imagine people showing such concern for a stranger. Well, after the meeting
ended, Naomi and Joseph, my Tibetan acquaintances, talked
to me about Jesus and what he had done for me, Wangden. I
felt a sense of openness, and my doubts disappeared. Very
quickly and simply I committed my life to Jesus. Then I
looked across the room and saw a woman whom I knew in
an instant. It was Hannah, the teacher that I had thrown
stones at in Batang!

"I got up and walked over to her. 'Were you ever in my
home town of Batang?' I asked.

'Yes', she replied, 'I spent a year there.'

"My second question was, 'Do you remember a school-
boy throwing stones at you and breaking up your meetings?'
And she smiled, 'Oh yes, I wouldn't forget that!'

"I took a deep breath and then told her, 'I was that boy.'
She got up, came over, and clasped my hands. 'You are!'
she exclaimed. 'Ever since then I've prayed for you. I
wanted the boy who opposed Jesus to find out how wonderful he is, believing such a boy would become a most loyal
disciple.'

"This experience totally changed my life. I enrolled at
the Bible school instead of going to the university. How my
fees would be met was not my major concern. I simply was
consumed with a burning curiosity to learn more about
Jesus Christ. As I listened to my teachers, my ambitions
changed. They taught me a better way to help my people,
starting with their hearts and showing them the love of Jesus
I had found."

When Wangden finished, I sat back in awe at the way

God had been preparing this young Tibetan to minister to his own people. I certainly wasn't indispensable. The cloud that had been gathering around our hopes and dreams for the "hourglass" valleys lifted at that moment. I could see that God had the situation under control. I could rest easy about whatever part remained for me in his grand plan. But the plan included Chinese and Tibetans, not just westerners. And that, of course, was as it should be and as we had always wanted it.

"Tell me about Mako," Wangden asked me.

"Well, he has grown rapidly as a Christian and very early said that he wanted to be a preacher to Tibetans," I replied. "Last fall he took a turn preaching in both Chinese and Tibetan services in Ganzi, and he helped start a small Sunday school. Every weekday afternoon he had a Tibetan Bible study. This January Margaret had a long talk with him about the meaning of Romans, the sixth chapter, about dying to sin and rising to a new life in Christ. He grasped what she was showing him and accepted it for himself then and there. The three ladies said there was an immediate change in his whole demeanor. He had been shy, not an outgoing evangelist like Lo at the post office. Mako is becoming more of a "people person", talking freely with strangers. I think you can be a big help to him, and he will certainly be ready to help you any way he can."

"Thanks. That's just what I wanted to know. I'm looking forward to meeting him and the others up there." Wangden left for Ganzi in May, 1949, expecting to return in a few months to Kangding. We soon began to receive welcome reports of fresh vigor in the Ganzi church. That was much more important to us than the fact that the Communists had crossed the Yangtse River and captured Nanjing.

Wangden galvanized the believers to buy benches for the church and to contribute money for the care of the poor. He sent me detailed letters about those "who could be counted on to be in their seats" and those "who were willing to witness." He had an attendance of around 30 for some special meetings he held, and for a work in a new area, not one year old, that was extraordinary.

CHAPTER 19

TO LEAVE OR TO STAY

When Betty and I arrived back in Kangding, I checked on our stock of tea in a local storehouse only to discover that it wasn't there. The merchant in charge told me he would have the tea for me in a few days. Obviously someone had been "speculating" with our tea, figuring on turning a profit from those idle stocks. But before the week was out, carriers arrived at our gate with every bit of our tea.

We were introduced more fully to the mysteries of silver coinage when the paper money completely collapsed. People had to dig up their secret savings from under the floorboards or in their back gardens. We could tell this by the discoloration of some of the coins that passed through our hands. It was essential to know how to distinguish the "big heads" from the "little heads" or the "big head with the closed eye"!

When our team was reunited, we had discussions about the changing situation and how we could continue to function should matters get worse. We wanted to "hang in there" if at all possible. If we made an exit by plane to Hong Kong, we wouldn't get back. In our new quarters on a ground floor, we often had eyes of passersby peeping through holes they made in our paper-covered windows. No matter how much we patched the paper, it would not stay intact for long. Our unwanted spectators wet the tip of a finger and gently pressed it on the thin paper. This would give them a perfect peephole. We finally paid no attention to our frequent audience though we did try to whisper if we wanted privacy. Our living room furniture was designed in Tibetan style, two long wooden platforms three feet wide, six feet long, and a foot and a half high. These we covered with colorful Tibetan rugs. Between these stood a set of three square tables, slightly higher. We had an iron pan set in a round hole in the center table, and this gave us a place for a cheery charcoal fire. For the first time we could lounge in true Tibetan fashion, but it wasn't very comfortable by Western standards. The platforms had no backs to lean against. They were made for sitting hunched forward and cross-legged, and we had made a start at living this way. Could we survive cut off from our supply channels in China?

To do so we still had to have supplies, and brick tea was the basic commodity all over Tibet. Transport costs would reduce 100 parcels of tea to 45 by the time a shipment reached Ganzi. The same shipment would shrink to 33 if sent to Chamdo where a Lhasa government tax would take a 50% slice. If we were to retreat into Tibet in the face of advancing Communists, we would have to deal with Tibetan trading companies and make payments in India. But what if our calculations were completely upset by a brand new set of circumstances? Suppose the trading companies and Tibetan government collapsed? Or we could face the risk of being robbed on the road, going through strange country. With women and a child to consider, that gave me pause.

"We are trying to decide what we should do," I said to Kesang, also called "the old teacher." He had traveled with us on our trip back from Batang, and occasionally I had taken Tibetan classes with him. "I used to go to a lama when

I needed to know what to do," he said with a playful chuckle, "that lama most of the time being myself!"

I knew that he had married and consequently left the priesthood, so I asked him how he found it as a monk. "I grew up right over the mountains here in Minya country, and my parents sent me to a monastery when I was ten years old. They sent me tsamba flour, cheese and butter regularly, and I had all I needed. Those lamas who taught us usually had about five or six students, and they could be very strict with them if they didn't pay attention. Some of my friends were orphans, and they preferred the monastery to living with relatives. I was often homesick but didn't dare run home. My father would have beaten me worse than my lama teacher.

"I would rate my home monastery as better than average. The standards were high, and priests that didn't make the grade were thrown out. My first work in the monastery was to sweep floors and pour tea. Then I learned to blow one of the long horns. To get to blow the shorter silver horns was considered a great privilege.

"The day came when I was ready to take my vows. I had to swear to serve Buddha and be a true priest, sanctified in mouth, body and heart. The last of these mean I would not be covetous and thus would not engage in trade."

I was surprised. "But I know lots of priests who are traders," I said.

"Most of the traders are really former priests who work for a monastery," Kesang told me. "When I took the vows, I was idealistic. For the first time I could add a yellow sash to my red robes and ties around my boots. I was very happy at that time. Whenever bad thoughts came to me, I would say to myself, 'I am a priest. I must not think these bad thoughts.'"

He paused. "What happened next?" I asked.

"I did so well that I was appointed steward. I was faithful in my accounts, but it disturbed me when I found out how the common people complained about their grain taxes to the monastery. I began to find out how they were suffering from trying to pay back the loans they took out from us. The interest was so high. It worried my conscience when I knew that the grain I was collecting for the monastery in some cases left poor farmers with nothing to plant in the spring.

"I began to think about leaving the priesthood because I didn't like what I was having to do. It was eight years before I left the monastery and took a wife. My fellow priests blamed me for marrying; they could not understand how I felt about the business of the monastery. Well, I took my wife and moved all the way to Batang. There at first I earned a bit reading scriptures, but when I gained a reputation as a teacher, I had enough students to care for my family. I was there for 16 years. Then I decided it was time to come back home."

He took a sip of tea. There was a sad look in his eyes. "My wife was so depressed. She blamed herself for spoiling my life. Nothing I could say would persuade her otherwise. This led to fits of insanity. Finally she jumped off a flat roof and broke her shoulder. I thought she needed to come back to her home country, and indeed she has improved since coming back. I keep her in the grasslands and she's content there. My daughter is getting more and more independent from being in a public school right here. I don't know how to handle her. I can't discipline her. My father would be shocked at how disrespectfully she talks to me!"

I looked at this man. He had a very fine head, a strong chin, and a straight nose. But there was a pallor about him that didn't look healthy. Only when we got into the intricacies of the Tibetan language was he transformed, his quick mind playing with words and ideas. "Thank you, Kesang, for telling me about your life," I said. How outstanding he was. I wondered what the future held for him. Then an idea struck me. "Do you think the 'anilas' (the three ladies of our team) could go out and visit you in Minya?" I asked. He assured me that they would be welcome any time they could come. Margaret and Edie had made a trip out that way two years before, and they wanted to take Hester to see the famous Minya Gonka, highest peak in eastern Tibet, from a close up vantage point.

A trip to the peaceful grasslands would be a relief from Kangding uncertainties. A man had been stabbed in the shoulder during a riot at one of the banks. Rumors had it that a bandit horde was moving up in our direction from the south. Three thousand government employees had been ordered to move down to Yaan, and the streets were filled with vendors trying to sell second-hand goods. Some stores were closing for lack of business, and the price of chairs and carriers had soared nine fold in a matter of weeks. Unable to pay such prices, many women trudged down to the plains on foot, placing their babies on top of coolie loads. It was a sad state of affairs.

"Some of us have simply got to go down to Chengdu," I told the ladies. "It's no pleasure trip; we need to make purchases and bring in silver dollars. The banks have just about had it!" Margaret decided to accompany Betty and me. We had debated the advisability of taking Marion, but felt it was too perilous for her. Since Hester and Edie were willing to take care of our daughter, we left her with them. It turned out to be a scary trip for us. We were attacked once by bandits, a bullet landing, "plonk", in the dirt beside me. A bus strike in Yaan forced us to travel the slow way by rickshaw to Chengdu, three days instead of one. I admired the way my rickshaw driver would speed downhill, his feet off the ground, his arms grasping the shafts, while I was tipped way back nearly flat as a result of this delicate balancing act. We were also rather sore after three days of bumping along. Near Chengdu a truck roared up behind us, and then stopped. In it were two Americans, part of a large group that had moved south from Shanxi some months before to escape the Communist armies. They invited us to ride with them which meant sitting high up in a jeep they had loaded on the back of the truck. We gladly paid the rickshaw men, and climbed aboard the truck and up into the jeep. From there we had a splendid view plus the comfortable jiggle of springs below us.

Soon after our arrival in Chengdu, we received a telegram from Edie telling us that Marion was seriously ill with bronchial pneumonia and her heart seemed to be giving out. We took the slip of paper into our bedroom and faced up to the reality that in this unexpected emergency there was no way we could get back to Kangding to be by the bedside of our daughter. As we prayed about this, God told us, "This sickness is not unto death." So by the time we came out of that room, we could tell our friends with confidence, "She's going to live." Twenty-four hours later we received another wire with the news that she was past the crisis.

Betty and Margaret did not delay but returned immediately to Kangding, leaving me to complete the business details. When Betty got back there, Marion was better. Hester poured out the story of what had happened. "When Marion began to get worse, I couldn't believe it," she told her. "I never dreamed this would happen while you were away. The crisis was quick, about 24 hours. I called the doctor, and she didn't think that Marion's heart would be strong enough to last the night. That's when we sent you the telegram! John Ding, his wife, and his mother-in-law, Mrs. Ju, came around to pray for Marion. Oh, I wish you could have heard them – so earnest – so full of faith! Even though Mrs. Ju's false teeth clack while she prays, she is a powerhouse! That evening Edie and I were still so concerned that we touched her forehead with the oil we had been using on her chest and prayed for her. The next morning when I went in, Marion was well, sitting up in bed and playing!"

Edie chimed in, "When the doctor came, she was

dreading what she might find. How her face lit up, and she said, 'This is a miracle!' Then she told us that she and her co-workers had prayers for Marion too."

"Well, I'm glad to accept all the help we could get," Betty laughed. "After all you've been through you girls ought to have a change. Why don't you make that trip to Minya country? It's almost spring." The ladies whooped with joy and began to talk about the trip, while Betty went over and cuddled Marion.

Down in Chengdu Lucille Chang was so helpful to me, and whenever I protested that she was doing too much, she reiterated that she enjoyed being part of what we were doing. "The Lord won't let me off the hook," she said. "I've been tempted to cut back, and he won't let me."

I took a box of silver coins back with me, and I couldn't help feeling very vulnerable with this small treasure. It was so obvious by its weight as to what it was. But in Yaan I was able to join other travelers who were carrying money into Kangding. We had a military escort, and at nights they set up a machine gun in the courtyard of whatever inn we were using. It was a relief to reach the gates of Kangding, for we could have been ambushed along the road.

I was in time to help the three single ladies get their caravan to visit Minya country. It was May when they set out, but they got more snow than they bargained for. As they struggled up Jezi Pass, the snow was blowing so heavily that they could see only a few feet ahead. At their campsite they were too tired to get wood for a fire. All they wanted was to get under shelter. Their companions had no tent, so they gave them a ground sheet for a cover. Other travelers came later, carrying wood, and that provided a fire. The next morning the ladies' tent was flapping, and they discovered that the men had made off with some of the tent pegs during the night, using them to hold down the tarpaulin under which they were sheltering. After this blizzard the ladies assumed they must have been close to the top of the pass only to find that they were still at the foot of the Jezi pass and had a climb through the snow ahead of them. When they reached the Jezi La, they had a fabulous view of sun and shadows chasing each other over the craggy peaks. The snow on the path was high, and the yak had to break the trail for their horses as they continued toward the grasslands.

All this to reach Minya and make some new friends. By this time, badly sunburned, eyes swollen, they could have been mistaken for patients! They had been on the road for eight days and were ready for a rest. But first they had the usual appeals for medicine. They had a dark, dirty room in a homestead next to a monastery. Several of the young priests came over to talk with these foreigners. One who spent much time listening to them was severely reprimanded by his head lama. One of the Tibetan women said to them with tears in her eyes, "I wish I could live a good life, but this valley is too wicked. I just couldn't live a good life here." The ladies mulled over this statement of hopelessness. Buddhism has a saying, "The bitter sea has no bounds. Repent, and the shore is at hand." Repentance alone wasn't working for this woman. Giving up her own efforts and seeking the Savior's help would. Like the young priest who came back and in haste assured them, "No matter what others say, I believe in Jesus in my heart." To them he had a light in his face as though he had reached salvation's shore.

Moving on to the old teacher's home, they found a warm welcome awaiting them. Kesang was the gracious host. "I didn't think you would make it," he said, "but I am honored that you would come so far over such rough roads. Visitors always bring news. Tell us about the friends down in Dardzendo (Kangding). How are conditions in the city?" They hastened to bring him up to date as best they could.

When it came to religious discussion, Kesang liked to

compare the similarities between Buddha and Christ. "I know that you Christians think that Jesus is the only Savior because He is the only Son and the only one who died for us. I think about that a lot. I may believe some day, but I'd rather come along gradually and not be pushed into it. I'm not like some who give assent with their mouths but don't believe in their hearts. But if I believe, it will be real."

When our team was together again, we talked over the Minya trip. "It was so obvious to us that in the hearts of some Tibetans there is a hunger for something better, for something different," said Edie.

"Yes," said Hester, "while many are completely indifferent, there are others who are searching for something more satisfying than what they now have."

"Let's keep going as long as we can," I said. "From what we hear of the Communist occupied areas, foreigners don't have much freedom of movement."

In June we heard that President Chiang Kai-shek had retired from the presidency, and his vice-president, Lee Tsung-jen, attempted to govern. Mail service stopped in many provinces of China, and for weeks we received no mail. We had decided to stay even under the Communists, so I suggested, "Some of us had better get back to Ganzi." We decided that I escort Margaret and Edie up there, and I would stay for a while and help the local church. Mako and Lozongdrema were rejoicing in the birth of a son. Born on my birthday, June 11, he was named for me. Hester would wait in Kangding with Betty for the arrival of the last member of the team. We were expecting Nellie, an experienced China hand, coming to us from England. As long as planes continued to fly into Sichuan, she could get in from Hong Kong. I would return in the fall, and then Hester could take Nellie up to Ganzi. Betty was expecting our second child in January, and Kangding was the best place for our family to be. These days we were aware that as soon as the

Communists did show up, we would be immobilized. Thus, we needed to get in place with the thought that wherever we were, we might be there for a long time.

CHAPTER 20

A CHURCH STARTS
TO GROW

W angden greeted me warmly at the clinic on my return
to Ganzi. "You'll be staying with me in an apartment
down the street," he told me. My eyes turned to the clinic
doors that had been freshly painted. Their bright red and
trim of green and blue now had an addition of scripture
verses in bright orange. The lettering was in both Tibetan
and Chinese.

"Beautifully done," I exclaimed. "Did you do it?"

"Mako and I did it together," he replied. "Oh, I wanted
to speak with you about him before you meet with him.
Let's walk down the road."

Wangden told me that when Mako did his accounts with
me regarding the 300 rupees I had left with him there would
be a shortage. "Let me intercede for him," Wangden said,
"You simply did not pay him enough, and, after all, he is
your employee. I advise you to cancel his debt, for I think
most of the problem came about with the extra expense of
his brother's visit. He has done a very good job in your
absence. I can speak for him and his faithfulness. He has

often gone up to Ganzi town with me to distribute tracts and do visitation, and he's enthusiastic about it."

Before I saw Mako about this matter I talked it over with Edie and Margaret, and they agreed that I should not try to collect the missing money. Mako was so relieved when I told him. He was like a tight spring uncoiling. Heaving a deep breath, "Oh, thank you." he said. Then he took my arm. "Come," he said, "let me show you our little Dawei!" Lozongdrema held the baby proudly, and I was suitably impressed by the chubby baby with rosy cheeks, who bore my name.

Wangden and I had a small apartment down the street, and we furnished two or three rooms sparsely. We were using the cots that I had originally received on the S. S. James Buchanan in the Bay of Calcutta. Our meals we had up at the clinic house. Wangden would get up early in the morning and go out for a walk. Striding down toward the river, he would sing at the top of his lungs and have his prayers. Not many people lived in the neighborhood, but such travelers as were already on the road got the full bene-fit of this strange "lama" having his devotions. He was as unconcerned about a public demonstration of his faith as any of his fellow Tibetans would be.

"We have five young men waiting for baptism," he told me. "Let's go out and have a look at the hot springs. It is too cold to use the millstream." I agreed, and we set out across the plain. Usually we expected to find hot springs on hill-sides or near them. This spring was in the middle of a flat pastureland. We, of course, took advantage of the chance for a bath in the black, steaming water. "It'll do." Wangden said, so we laid our plans for a church picnic out by the spring for the following Sunday.

The fall weather was promising the next weekend, but once we set up the tent we had brought to the spring, we heard the roll of thunder, the whistle of a rising wind, and we saw heavy mists blot out our sight of the towering snow peaks. A storm was approaching, and Wangden supervised our preparations. From above we would have looked like pygmy figures, running around tightening tent ropes and pounding in pegs. Within the white tent we had rugs spread on the ground, and a tea churn over by the door flaps. We could hear the rising roar from the campfire outside as the wind raged at it, and the three Tibetan women tending the fire tried to build a windbreak. A wall of rain was coming toward them, and it might finish the fire off.

Then "rip" went the tent, and the billowing cloth slumped to the ground on top of those of us within. With a great thrashing we emerged one by one, laughing and shouting. Mako rushed over to a neighboring tent of three priests and got the loan of some sewing materials, came back, and began to repair the damage. When done, he called for help, and everybody gave a hand in getting the flapping tent back up. Our fingers were numbing; our shoes filled with water. What a relief to get in the shelter from the wind. True, the interior was a shambles. We were a disheveled looking lot. No matter, for now we had hot butter tea to drink and hunks of bread to go with it. As bowl after bowl were refilled, our spirits and talk revived. We were ready for the baptisms, but most of our group watched from the doorway of the tent.

In a pouring rain and needling wind, Wangden and I waded out into the tepid waters of the spring. Our teeth were chattering, and the water no noticeable comfort. One by one the new believers hurried out and were baptized. The lamas peered out of their tent at this extraordinary sight. Ridiculous? Well, not really. One of these young men made a point of standing up in one of our next meetings and saying, "I was touched to see the two pastors willing to get so cold and wet so that we could be baptized."

One young Chinese in that number was transferred West to Dege, and within two months we were shocked by the tragic news that he had been falsely accused and shot dead in his own bedroom. It did force us to ask Wangden what he thought about this Brother Chou's spiritual condition. But Wangden was firm in his belief in his sincerity. "He would have had to be a pretty good actor to fool me," he said. "I look for signs of spiritual reality and am sensitive to anything false." At this time Mao Zedong had just announced in Beijing the founding of the People's Republic of China. Then before the end of 1949 President Chiang and his Nationalist government would have moved to Taiwan. As a result the American Consulate in Chungqing would notify us that it was closing. In Ganzi we already sensed what was coming and the decisions we soon would have to make. For the present at our station it was the calm before the storm, but just like the tempest that had borne down on us at the hot springs, we knew the climate in Kham could change suddenly.

I found it remarkable that Wangden, a Tibetan, could be so acceptable to so many Chinese believers. To me it was an indication of how the animosity between these two peoples can be bridged. When we Christians gathered together, we were one family regardless of our racial background. Most of the church was made up of Chinese. In fact, there were 22 of them in membership by the end of the year. Most of the Tibetan converts were wives of believers. For example, the soldier, whose gunshot wound the previous year had threatened him with amputation, was so happy when he gradually healed that he listened carefully to Edie and Margaret and believed. His Tibetan wife was equally receptive.

One day a Chinese woodcutter came to see the ladies. Years before, he had suffered from cataracts on his eyes and was a beggar in Kangding. He was operated on at the Christian hospital and received his sight back. Able to work again, he had drifted up the north road. This day he came straight to the point. "I have come to accept Jesus and become a Christian," he declared. "I have already thrown away my idols and charms. My Tibetan wife and children are willing to believe, too. Tell me what to do."

Margaret smiled and lifted up a piece of paper. "Look and see what I am going to do with this," she told him. His eyes followed her as she slipped the paper into her Bible, and it was gone from sight. "You're like that piece of paper, Mr. Gao," she said. She took it out again. "When this paper is in that book, it is secure. Nothing can reach it. And when you are in God's care, you are secure." She put the paper into the Bible, and he said, "Oh, then the devil can't find me!" He understood, and he was overjoyed. This led to his bringing a second woodcutter. This man had heard what Jesus had done for his friend. Then in the night when he was struck by a piercing stomachache, he tried to pray to this same Jesus. All he could think of doing was to call out the name. When he did, the pain immediately left! He was so thrilled that he came to Edie and Margaret and handed over his amulet bags, dropping them in the charcoal fire. Then he remembered that he had a hair of a lama in his pocket as a charm. He brought that out, too, and dropped it on the coals.

The ladies checked out these woodcutters' families for amulets. Finding one on a small baby just three months old, Edie asked, "What's that for?" The Tibetan woman replied, "It is to help the baby's hair to grow."

"You take it off," Edie said, "and I'll guarantee you that the baby will have lots of hair without that." So it, too, shriveled up in the flames.

For a week I had daily talks with a monk who was visiting in Ganzi. Gendun was a young man, full of questions but also grasping at answers. Before long he took off his amulets, admitting that he had no faith in them. Persisting, he declared that he had faith that Jesus was the only Savior who had ever provided a sure way to be rid of sin. "I believe as you do," he told me, "and I would take off these red robes, but they are the only clothes I have." When he was ready to return home, he thanked me for helping him to faith. I promised to pray for him, and then he walked slowly out into the plain. He lived off the main road, and I never had the opportunity to visit him in his hidden valley home. Wangden, however, assured me that Gendun was very clear in his faith.

I had further opportunities with Dawa Dongdrup, the trade agent of a ruling family in Rombatsa valley. He came over to see me. "Oh," he said, "I wanted to believe in Jesus when I was a student in Darjeeling. My relatives heard of my interest and took me out of school. But I'm on my own now, and I can make my own decisions. Help me. I want to be sure that I am a Christian." He came through very clearly to a place of faith, but he said, "It will be a lonely life for me, for I go back where there are no Christians. But I know that I can talk to Jesus and read his word so I won't be alone. The people I work for would not understand if I told them I am a Christian."

"Don't be so sure about that," I replied. "Someone will ask you someday why you have such peace, why you are full of joy. And you will need to explain. Don't hold back when you have a chance like that."

The weeks slipped by so quickly, and then it was time for me to return to Kangding. Wangden intended to go along with me in order to join the two Britishers heading for inner Tibet. We were grateful for having him in Ganzi almost six months. What a strong preacher he was! He would be missed. When Mr. Lo, assistant at the post office, approached us, asking if his wife with their baby son could join us on the trip, we were glad to be of help. In October we secured animals in a caravan and would be traveling light.

The trip to Daowu was fast, but the weather was getting cold. The little child had developed a cold which concerned me. Travelers warned us of a band of seven armed bandits who leveled their guns at them, but then turned away after seeing they were outgunned. The caravan we met then passed the bandits unmolested. We mounted the heavily wooded pass south of Daowu alert for danger, but we had no trouble there. The cold wind was beating across the table-lands beyond, and the Lo baby was getting sicker and sicker. Mrs. Lo told us he was dying, and we asked the caravan men to stop. Quickly, I erected my tent, and Mrs. Lo sheltered in it with the little boy. It was not long, however, before he died. Wangden and I conducted our first Christian funeral in Tibet, and I provided a winding sheet for the little body. The caravan men suggested a nearby cave for the burial, and we piled up rocks before its entrance. Then in a matter of minutes we were into our saddles and on our way lest the darkness catch us in that wilderness.

When we came down over Jeddo pass and into Kangding, just about the first news we heard was that George and Geoff, the two British men, had left with the great Kham chieftain, Panda Dorje, and were headed West already. Wangden was bitterly disappointed to be left behind. Could they have assumed he was so involved at Ganzi that he had perhaps given up the original plan? Or had they left so abruptly they couldn't notify him? Wangden acted like he was in a daze. He didn't feel that he could chase after them uninvited. He didn't know what he should do. He could go home to Batang but didn't want to do that. One day I talked with him, saying, "Brother, you know you would always be welcome back in Ganzi. Why don't you consider going back there to work?" Some days later he told me, "I'm going back to Ganzi. I feel at peace about that."

Our sixth team member, Nellie Stokes, had arrived by plane from Hong Kong. She was able to outfit herself very well with the gifts of some other foreigners in the city who had left for Hong Kong. Then Hester, Nellie, and Wangden took a caravan to Ganzi, taking young Mrs. Lo with them. When they passed the spot where her son had been buried, they were shocked to find the cave broken open and the body gone. Only the winding sheet lay out on the field below the grave. Wild animals had done their job thoroughly, and this young mother was doubly crushed. As they went along, she explained to Nellie that she was afraid Mr. Lo would blame her for the death of their son. "I haven't met your husband," Nellie said, "but from what I have heard about him, I don't think he would act that way. He loves you too much for that." Mrs. Lo's fears were groundless, for Mr. Lo was understanding and a great comfort to her. Wangden explained to him all about the baby's illness, death and burial that had happened on the way down to Kangding, and Mr. Lo was comforted.

Mako met Wangden with a broad smile. "I'm so glad you returned," he said. "You've taught me so much, and I want to learn more." This enthusiastic welcome made Wangden realize he had found his niche, his field of service right there in Ganzi.

Reading the Gospel in Tibetan

CHAPTER 21

IN THE VORTEX OF
A STORM

The reason we received Nellie Stokes to join our team at this late date was because her intended route to China's northwest had been cut. She was in Hong Kong and desperately wanted to get back into China before entry would be denied to foreigners. So we wired her to come and join us.

Hester, Nellie, and Wangden made off for Ganzi just in time. Chungqing had fallen to the Communist armies, and Chengdu, our nearest large city, was threatened. The caravan had barely left when our own Kangding garrison defected to the Communists in advance of any Communist authorities to accept their surrender. Our cook gave us this news with an expressionless face. Coming in for work, she announced, "Kangding is under the Communists now." When we pressed Yeshe for explanations, she told us, "Governor Liu Wen-hui sent the officials here orders to surrender to the Communists, and of course they obeyed him. But they don't know what to do".

Soldiers replaced the blue and white Nationalist sun emblem on their caps with a red star, and I saw one confused private wearing both sun and star! Nationalist flags disappeared overnight, and the red flag flew over government buildings. Some townsfolk simply cut out the corner sun from their flags and sewed in a field with the large star for the Han people and a crescent of four small stars to represent the minorities of China. Paper slogans favoring the revolution began to appear on walls around the city, but much was in a holding pattern, waiting for Communist troops to arrive.

Betty and I were waiting for the arrival of our second child in January, 1950. Betty hurried to complete a Tibetan exam and get it out of the way. Then we decided to make a house move to give ourselves more room. The new house was just several doors down the lane, so I hired three men for $5.00, and they transferred all of our goods and chattels. I had the satisfaction of knowing that a group of women tea carriers who had asked for ten times as much for the job would learn I had gotten a better bargain. Electricians had to transfer all wiring, switches, and meter, for renters owned these themselves. As they were preparing to leave, I checked and found the kitchen switch would not work. They laughed and tinkered with the switch until the light blinked on. The next day it was no longer functioning and I had to fix it myself. That was par for the course.

Betty and I were pleased to be in a larger and more private building. We would have no more eyes at the paper-covered windows. We would have to get used to the door-sills at every doorway, standing eighteen inches high! Within a day Betty admitted, "I've bruised my shin already. But perhaps they will have some value. I know they'll keep out the cold drafts as well as slow Marion down." Marion had a cold which cleared up nicely in the new surroundings, and that meant that everything was ready for son Ted's appearance in the new maternity section at the Catholic hospital on January 20. I was present beside Betty for the births of both Marion and Ted because Sister Miriam, the nurse, held strongly to the opinion that husbands needed to know what their wives endured in giving birth.

At this time the veteran missionary, Mrs. Cunningham, of the China Inland Mission, was bedfast and failing. When she heard that the Woodwards had a new son with a shock of red hair, she waved her hand feebly and smiling said, "Red...red...we've got a lot of red around here these days!" Two weeks later she died and was buried up on the hillside beside her husband. Our cook, Yeshe, and many other young people called her "Teacher" because she had taught them to read, to knit, and to cook. Mrs. "C" had always loved flowers, and now in the middle of winter, among all the paper flowers, on her grave lay a spray of some fresh flowers she had tended herself.

One day that winter a Ganzi caravan man rapped at our gate and we welcomed him in. After serving him tea, I asked if he had passed any foreign ladies on his trip down to Kangding.

"No," he replied, "but you know there are many different routes below Dawu. We could easily have missed them."

After some more small talk he got around to asking me if we had any loads we would like to have him take up to Ganzi. I welcomed the opportunity. Obviously he had not been able to find sufficient loads elsewhere, probably due to the chaotic conditions prevailing. This man, Sonam, was a day ahead of his caravan, and was lining up business for an immediate turnaround. I talked to Betty about the dried carrots and potatoes we had in large tins. They weren't very appetizing, but in a pinch the ladies might be glad to have them. We counted up the brick tea and Chinese noodles and figured we could prepare five loads in the 24 hours Sonam was giving us. The price was one and a half packets of tea for a load of brick tea, two packets for heavier boxes. I gave him some pictures for his five-year-old son, Drashi, and he left all smiles. This shipment was the next to last we were able to send to the ladies in Ganzi because most caravans stopped coming into Kangding during the next six months. Tibetans feared they would lose their animals and with good reason. Chinese armies had a penchant for wanting transport, so ordinary trade would have to wait. In these abnormal conditions, I decided to sell my gold watch in order to raise some funds. Betty was dubious, but I told her, "I haven't used it since I got one of those Swiss watches Lucille sent in from Chengdu. I'll approach Tupchen, the trader, about it."

He wondered, no doubt, what brought me around, but when I dangled the watch in front of him, his eyes sparkled. "How much are you asking?" he said to me. I replied, "Thirty bao (packets) of good quality tea."

He countered with an offer of 23 bao, and we settled for 27 "delivered to the door". Tupchen broke open the rattan casing on several packets and showed me the tea and the paper labels. Yeshe and our other helper, Karma, were experts at checking and would do a more careful examination on delivery. The tea carriers labored up the rough, cobbled path outside our door and brought their loads into our storeroom. When all the tea had been checked and stacked, I gave it a kick with my boot and said to Betty, "That certainly qualifies as hard currency."

"I want you to get a new jacket," she said.

"I will if you get some wool for a new Tibetan robe," I replied. And that is how we spent some of our tea, buying good quality cloth from Britain, brought across Tibet from India.

The troops in Kangding then fled to the grasslands when they heard that 3,000 loyal Nationalist troops were coming over the mountains from Guanxian. Some high-ranking officials also fled, commandeering mule caravans to take their personal property to a place of safety, very upset that they had misjudged and jumped to the other side too soon. Some other garrisons in southern Sikang province had had the caution not to follow the governor's precipitate instructions. These fleeing soldiers had pieces of red paper stuck to their rifles to indicate that their loyalties were with the People's Republic. Their uniforms, however, were still the old Nationalist ones. What confusion!

An hour after the last stragglers trailed out past our gate the Nationalist troops entered on the other side of the city. The red flags had disappeared; the posters were being ripped down. The local people had firecrackers ready to welcome the newcomers as well as food to feed them. The forerunners banned the firecrackers for fear that they could cloak some opposition rifle fire. They would be glad to requisition food and lodging as required. We heard of some cases of looting from the governor's mansion and government offices. The newly arrived forces soon realized that the city simply could not provide them with sufficient supplies, so they radioed to one of the few remaining Nationalist strongholds, pleading for an air drop.

We had not realized what was going on, but one day we heard a strange hum. Startled, we went out into our garden, and looking up, saw a plane pass over the city. When white parachutes blossomed and drifted down into the valley outside the south gate, we realized what was happening. It was the first plane we had seen in years. Did it spell new hope for the Nationalists? Hardly, because it was too little and too late to save this army.

The next morning Yeshe and Karma did not come for work. Puzzled, I started the charcoal fires by myself. As I was fanning the brazier outside, I could hear the clatter of hooves as well as voices on the other side of the wall. Peering out, I saw a stream of humanity, each person with a roll of bedding and some other possessions, all heading out of the city. It could mean only one thing – that the

Nationalists were abandoning Kangding and that the PRC troops were approaching. People simply didn't want to be around when the takeover came because they didn't know what to expect. In some cases, men sent their families out of the city and up on the hillsides until it was safe for them to return. Mingled among these refugees were Nationalist soldiers. I remember one of them, chopsticks in hand, eating a last bowlful of rice as he walked slowly along. Some of these men eventually reached Burma and years later were repatriated to Taiwan. But for the present in Kangding, tins of Taiwan pineapple were going for a song. That is where President Chiang and the Nationalist government had gone. No merchants wanted to have Taiwan products on their shelves, and they were eager to get rid of this stock as soon as possible.

The Communist troops arrived the same day that the Nationalist troops pulled out and retreated to the grasslands. I was down on one of the main streets when I saw a detachment of soldiers, coming toward me at a steady, determined pace. I could see the stars on their caps. This was the real thing. With their rubber shoes they came surprisingly quietly. I decided that was enough sightseeing on my part, and I returned to our compound. If there was going to be any billeting, I had better be home to deal with it. That didn't happen to us, but it would to the ladies up in Ganzi.

The next day Yeshe and Karma arrived at their usual time, and they assured us that this "liberation army" was well-behaved. "They aren't taking anything," Yeshe said, "and they are acting very polite."

"They call older people 'uncle' or 'auntie'," said Karma. "They are telling them to give the army suggestions how best to get things in order. And we learned that if any of these soldiers harms one of the common people, he gets severely punished!"

Instead of acting like conquerors and taking advantage

of the residents, these soldiers were well supplied and went about their business without interfering with the daily life of the people. They slung tarpaulins across the streets and provided their own shelter.

The local monks were surprised when the Communists came to them with money to pay for special ceremonies to commemorate the comrades who had died on their way to Kangding. "Buy butter for the butter lamps." they were exhorted. "Brothers, if this isn't enough, we'll give you more."

It didn't take long for the citizens who had fled the city to come back and witness these extraordinary people – so different from the Long March troops long before or some recent Nationalist troops. This was the era of goodwill and great expectations. But those of us who were aware of changing patterns down-country kept repeating the Chinese saying, "First, the nod of the head, second, the shake of the head, and lastly, off with the head." We were at "stage one" when little of the old order was being challenged. The Tibetans were not to be alarmed while preparations went forward to enter Tibet. China was going to settle the question of Tibet by the simple expedient of gaining authority over it.

Bookstores were among the first shops to reopen, and their shelves were filled with Communist literature. To provide for more locally produced news sheets two printing presses in the city were activated. One of them was right next to us and had not been in use for years. When we heard the first clanks and whams of the machinery, we were startled. We had other surprises in store. When I attended a mass gathering in front of the main government building, whom did I see in a prominent place on the platform but our water carrier, who daily brought us pails of water with a carrying stick over his shoulder. We had two large wooden water containers in our central hall, and he would make trip after trip until they were filled. Now it dawned on me that he must be a prominent local leader. Would surprises never end for us in this brand new China we lived in? Orderly, methodical, and purposeful. We felt that another aspect of the puzzle fell into place because of what we heard about a man named Ma Yuen-lung. He had become a Christian believer in the local prison two years before. This was the result of Ed Beatty's prison visitation. Ma responded to Ed's friendship and message which was most unusual because Ma was a Moslem. Ed baptized him along with some other prisoners right within the confines of the prison. On release, Ma went home to his wife, but she rejected him at the instigation of an enraged Moslem community. Ed invited him to live in the gatehouse at the China Inland Mission, and he earned a living as an itinerant trader. One day he visited Ed and insisted on a seat facing the window. "Someone might be behind those bushes," he said. "Listen, I have to be careful. For years I was a Communist and worked hard for the Party. Now that they have come and are in power, they are asking me to become active again. They tell me I can have my pick of jobs because of my former service for them. But I have no desire to be a Communist cadre or official. I am going to reject their offer. I am a Christian, and I know that sooner or later this will become an irreconcilable issue with them."

Two days later Ed Beatty's wife, Marjorie, observed two soldiers leading Ma away under arrest. His testing had begun and we prayed earnestly for this ardent believer. When Ed tried to visit him in prison, he was barred from entry. Ma shortly was dragged out for public execution, both his legs broken. He was charged with trying to escape and other crimes. The Communists were killing a man they had trained and who had no objection to socialism. But something else had been added to his life, a higher loyalty that they could not manage or cope with. For us who had known this brave and good man, his death showed us a tremendous faith to the end.

Communist planes began to fly over the city and drop supplies, but instead of aiming at a flat area outside the city the drops came right down on top of us! The first time this happened Betty and I were standing near the chapel when we heard a "Whoom!" and something hit the chapel roof, sending up a cloud of dust and broken tile. It was only afterwards that we sighted the plane, flying so high that it was soundless. Sacks of rice continued to drop, without parachutes, and they looked like bombs as they came down on the city. It was crazy! Because of injuries and alarm among the populace, a local official came to our door later and warned us to stay inside should the planes return. They were dropping sacks of rice, and these could be lethal. Miss Wang, a good friend of ours, was sitting with two of her orphan children in their bedroom when another bunch of bags were dropped over the city. Two bags of rice came crashing through her roof, landing beside them and leaving them unharmed.

Another afternoon Betty and I looked out our windows into the garden, having noticed two girls there staring upwards. All of a sudden they began to run in a panic, and a bag of rice fell between them, splitting on a rock! Injury cases were beginning to flood into the hospital, and at last the word must have gone down to Sichuan to halt these dangerous deliveries. From that time on we would see the planes high in the sky, but they continued on and dumped their supplies on the wide Ganzi plain. The Tibetan Communist party had been founded at Ganzi in 1935 during the Communists' Long March. Some Tibetan youth had been swept into the Communist armies, and now fifteen years later were being sought out in various parts of China to reassemble as a Tibetan regiment to be formed in Ganzi. They would then assault inner Tibet.

The average Chinese foot soldier was unaware of the rigors that lay ahead in Tibet. Some of them were northerners accustomed to cold, but they had never been at high altitudes. When I talked with one footsore youth, sitting on a curb and nursing his blister, he looked up at me and said hopefully, "It's only another week's march on the road to Lhasa, isn't it?" To his disappointment I told him it would be two or three months.

One detachment moved into the grasslands to supervise road construction. They were so decimated by sickness that the whole unit had to be withdrawn. They were hurried through Kangding by night and it seemed that the new government wisely didn't want anyone to be discouraged by the condition they were in. The Tibetan weather had won the first round, but the military would learn how to survive in the rugged terrain.

CHAPTER 22

EATING HUMBLE PIE

S oon after the arrival of the Communists in force in
Kangding valley it became apparent to us foreigners
that we were not wanted. This was in part because Chinese
intervention in the Korean War made Americans enemy
aliens. Also we were affected by being observers of a major
military campaign. Main streets were clogged with trucks.
Chinese troops were bivouacked in smaller alleys, stretching tarpaulins overhead from houses on one side to another.
We were in a restricted zone, and soon Ganzi was included
in this area.

The two Britishers in Batang decided to go westward,
George Patterson heading for India while Geoffrey Bull got
permission to go to Qamdo. The only other missionaries left
in the area were a young couple, newly arrived at Batang
and still in language study. The Backs were living on the
mission compound with their two children. When they
heard how Patterson had escaped, they decided to follow the
route George had taken to India. A crowd of young people,
eager for change and job opportunities, came out from town
and insisted on inspecting their baggage. The young
American man was struck down. Phillip, who accompanied

us on our first trip, interceded with the young hotheads, many of them his former classmates in the Batang elementary school. They grudgingly let the caravan leave, with Phillip again escorting foreigners who needed his help. It was a good thing he was along because they had a frightful trip. A severe earthquake blocked or ruined the usual trails and changed the course of rivers. By the time the party reached the Indian border Mrs. Back was in such bad shape that her husband, leaving the children in Phillip's charge, rushed his wife ahead for medical treatment. Because of the havoc the earthquake had created, Phillip was left with the two children for several weeks. They all eventually reached America where Phillip completed his education. He married an American and returned to India where he has been in church work ever since in the foothills of the Himalayas, a Tibetan missionary to India.

The ladies in Ganzi got the full impact of the military buildup for the invasion of Tibet. They noticed the increasing number of military in tents out on the plain. Edie and Margaret had been out planting in their garden and on their return home noticed some Chinese officers talking to the landlord, Ma. He turned to them and said, "The military want to speak with you. They need your house, and you can move into my house."

An officer spoke up, "You can understand this is an emergency, and we need your cooperation."

An air force group was commandeering the clinic house, and Mr. Ma had agreed to give the ladies three rooms in his own house. They were ordered to make the move in 24 hours. The next day when Nellie Stokes, who wasn't feeling well, had not moved out of her room, an officer, brushing aside Hester's requests for more time, simply said, "If she doesn't get out of this room today, we'll carry her out!"

A soldier explained to them, "You must suffer for what America is doing in dropping germs over our province of

Shandung." This charge had been made over and over in the Chinese press. Quietly and quickly they all made the move.

More Chinese troops poured into Ganzi valley, so every house had its quota of soldiers. Food immediately became scarce. The ladies had little space or privacy, with soldiers passing through their quarters, in and out, all day and late at night.

Wangden had from the start been an independent worker in Ganzi, not receiving any financial help from the foreigners. This was in his favor now because he could claim to have no contractual relationship with the four ladies. He had been thinking about his future and decided that he ought to have an occupation the military would regard as useful. He told Margaret that he was negotiating to buy a water mill, and that he would be moving there. When the ladies discovered that he had borrowed money from the monastery in order to swing the deal, they pointed out to him that the monastery might soon find all its money-lending under intense scrutiny. "We're going to be leaving soon," they said. "Help us to sell some of our things, and you can have the proceeds as a gift." Thus he secured the mill without any indebtedness. Because of the tremendous influx of Chinese, he was busy grinding grain at the mill and making a success of it financially. The military at that time paid well and promptly when they were dealing with the Tibetans. Moreover, Wangden also had the advantage of speaking fluent Chinese.

The ladies themselves bartered odds and ends for a little milk here and a few eggs there. They were way down in rations and rupees when I finally got a shipment through to them in June of 1950.

The ladies continued to offer medical care in their extremely crowded facilities, getting Tibetans and occasion Chinese patients. As a goodwill gesture they had made a gift of medicines to the Communist medical unit, and as a result a general came by to inspect their operation. He was not particularly impressed, but then not much was out in plain view. Nor was he pleased that they wore Tibetan gowns. "You ought to wear more modern clothes," he told them. Edie's reputation for tooth extractions brought her a good number of soldiers. Hester was also advising the princess, the Kangsa Bemo, regarding her latest pregnancy.

And what of old friends among Tibetans and Chinese? These meetings had to be fewer in number. Everybody was trying to get adjusted to a completely new and unfamiliar environment. Also there were regulations prohibiting large gatherings. The man who had lost, then found his pigs visited the foreigners. And on the road the man who prayed as he was falling from his horse came up and spoke with them. These people were of simple but practical faith, and they were finding satisfaction and freedom from fear in spite of the pressures they, too, were experiencing because of the revolution.

By this time the most entrenched among the foreigners in China were beginning to admit that the new regime did not want them around. Business people, educators, physicians and even missions themselves were beginning to revise their policies and evacuate personnel. The good news in Kangding was that the first missionary couple since "the liberation" had received their exit permits. The Beattys were allowed to leave, but not before a careful police search of their baggage. The inspector removed a Tibetan grammar from Ed's bag perhaps for his own Tibetan study or because he felt he had to take something. To witness two of our number leave was encouraging because we knew of many foreigners across China who were still denied exit permits. All of us had begun to recognize that we were a handicap to our local friends. We had stayed to encourage them, but now we knew we ought to leave. "I thought I was going to spend my life in Tibet," said Betty, "but God must want us out of the way. We're too controversial to be of much help except through prayer."

"One step at a time," I counseled, "but we really don't know the future. We can't figure out what's going to happen in the long run. From what we're hearing from Ganzi about crowded living conditions there, we had better try and get the ladies back here. They are less and less able to function there. If they request a move in this direction, I think they'll get permission. I think the military will be delighted to send them at least this far."

This was a difficult decision because we all knew that if they ever left Ganzi, they would not receive permits to return there. It would be the beginning of the end; that is, our winding down of the team's activities. As far as the government was concerned, we could move in only one direction and that was toward Hong Kong – and at their timing.

Looking back, I congratulate the ladies for the smooth way in which the six of us managed our affairs and our team relationships. Betty and I were younger than the four single ladies, but they accepted my leadership. I cannot recall a single unpleasantness during the whole time we worked together. Occasional differences of opinion, yes, but handled with mutual consideration and graciousness. I am sure that with the kind of external stresses we had that we didn't need the drag of internal strife. Instead we had bonded together.

Because of the ladies' shortage of food supplies in Ganzi they wouldn't be able to hold out much longer. I asked them to find out if Mako and Lozongdrema would be interested in returning to Batang. If so, we should take care of their moving costs. I felt that they would be more secure back in their home surroundings. Mako was smart and well trained, and he should be able to find some type of employment. They agreed to the move and were able to travel with the four ladies when they received permission to move down to Kangding.

Some of the Chinese Christians in Kangding had long since excused themselves from attending formal church services. They didn't want to be in formal church roles. For them it was a familiar step back to the house church type of worship many of them were already familiar with.

I heard a rap one day at our gate. "The foreigners' caravan from Ganzi is coming down from Jeddo," was the message. I told Betty, and then started walking out to meet our people. At last I spotted them in a field. Why would they be camping this far out of town? I noticed soldiers in uniform, and when I tried to approach the campsite, they barred my way. "Go no further," I was told, "This caravan is being inspected, and it will be released after a while. But you have no business here. Go back to the city!"

Regretfully I had to wave to all four of the ladies from a distance and walk back into Kangding. Betty, with the help of Yeshe and Karma, was making preparations for their arrival. The building we had rented had a second floor that would accommodate the party. What they would most enjoy would be a good home-cooked meal.

Several hours later they came, and what a story they had to tell us. "Coming down from Jeddo Pass we were surprised to have soldiers come out of the bushes and start walking alongside our horses," Edie said. "They didn't call it an arrest, but we were in the custody of forty soldiers. They told us that they had come to protect us! We had to camp out there overnight, and today we were inspected. It took us seven hours! They had two uniformed women give us a thorough body search. They even looked through our braided hair," Edie added. "If they were expecting to find anything precious or suspicious, they must have been disappointed."

"Maybe they were after your 'built-in radar'," I replied and told them about the unintentional phrase in a letter. "Whatever they were after, they had to find it out for themselves," Margaret said. "Our caravan men refused to open anything for them. These Tibetans were furious at the delay, just standing by, muttering their prayers and telling their beads. The military had to slash through the skin coverings themselves in order to get at our boxes. That is why it took so much time."

A few days later when a young police officer came to our house, he introduced himself to me as "Chen" and began to question me. Our ladies from Ganzi told me, "That's the same man who was in charge of our inspection out on the Jeddo road.

Well, Chen continued to drop in on me for an hour almost every day for months, interrogating me and rephrasing old questions. He must have built a voluminous file on me as he wrote out his daily reports.

Mako and Lozongdrema were with us about a week before we found a caravan for them, heading for Batang. "I've been exercising Dongwa," I told Mako. "You know what a good watchdog he is. He is yours if you want him, and I believe that he is in good enough shape to make the trip to Batang with you. That is, if you want him."

"Oh, I do," he exclaimed with pleasure. Dongwa had been the envy of every Tibetan I had met, so rare he was with his white color! He was full-size and a magnificent specimen. Three years old, our pet would be happier with people like Mako and Lozongdrema, whom he knew well.

"I want you to take one of our saddles for Lozongdrema," I added. We went ahead with their preparations, and one day we waved them off on the road west, Lozongdrema holding little David, Dongwa thrilled to be out on the trail again. He was romping ahead without a backward glance. Mako gave me a last wave, and they were gone.

Letting go, that's what we were being forced to do. But we were not the only ones making major adjustments. What of the well-to-do Chinese ladies selling their valuables for a pittance to raise funds to get back down-country? Their finery was no longer in style. We didn't buy much from these street side sales, but we were pleased to get a small sheepskin gown with silk cover for Marion. No Chinese child would have been seen in that dressy garment any longer, and we would not have paraded her in it outside. But certainly it kept her warm and comfortable around home.

A Tibetan woman told us one day, "I can see that soon we won't be able to trust even our best friend."

"What do you mean by that?" Margaret asked her.

"Simply that all of us are being told to report on one another, for the good of the cause, of course."

"And you think your best friend might betray you?" said Hester.

"Well, maybe not yet. But already we are afraid that if someone has a grudge against us, she could tell a lie about us. And there is no way we could defend ourselves. It is terrible when you begin to suspect members of your own family. Did you hear that Teacher Kesang's daughter has accused him, her own father?" That was unexpected news to us and gave us much food for thought. Were we open for accusation, too?

The revolution was affecting the closest of relationships. Here was Kesang, one of our teachers, in prison because the daughter he had doted on had turned on him. What sort of way was this to reward his love and care for her?

Hester and Edie were saddened to get news from Ganzi that the Tibetan princess had died in childbirth. Hester wished desperately that she could have been there to help. "Perhaps it need not have happened," she sighed. "But then, we had no choice but to come when we did."

"Those poor motherless children," Margaret remarked. We had also heard that their father had been taken away to Beijing to receive training. The new government must have thought that he would be useful to them in building a new Tibet.

CHAPTER 23

THE LOSS OF FREEDOM

When our team came to the decision to leave China, that choice was no longer ours. After filing our applications for exit permits, I made what I thought would be a routine trip to the police station to ask permission to send some of our heavier baggage ahead of us to Chengdu, using a transport company. The Communist cadre behind the desk issued a brief refusal and would not give me any explanation. It didn't look promising to me for an early departure on our part.

"Now what does it signify?" Betty asked, as we all discussed the situation. "No one here has been turned down before. You would think they would be glad to get rid of us."

"I don't know what is behind it," I replied, "but if we can't send our baggage, it is not likely that the police will issue the travel permits we applied for."

The August days passed, and then September 1950. We heard nothing further about exit permits. In fact, we learned that other foreigners in southwest China were having difficulty getting their exit permits. We were notified to come to the police station to fill out our residence registration papers. Friends in Chengdu had already done this once and were already getting renewals on their registration cards. Edie Seager voiced what we had all begun to realize, "We missed the easy time last spring before the local government got organized. Now it looks like we're going to be caught up in all the formalities before they let us leave."

In the process of registration the official who was processing me noticed that my passport had expired. He pointed this out to me, and I explained that the American Consulate in Chungqing had closed. "That will not do," he told me, "You are now here illegally. You will have to stay in your house because you have no right to be in the streets."

I knew that a number of the French priests in Kangding and elsewhere were being detained in their residences. Now I was in the same position as well as subject to daily interrogations from Policemen Chen from the Foreign Affairs Bureau.

He came like clockwork. I could count on him arriving about ten in the morning and staying an hour. He had a wide-ranging curiosity about my life, my friends, and my purpose for being in China. "Why did you go to India? Do you speak Russian? Do you speak French?" In the midst of these probing questions he maintained that he was simply making a casual visit with no particular purpose in mind. He would comment, "You seem to have a lot of leisure time." I decided to have some work to do whenever he came, chiefly unstitching clothing with a razor blade. I would listen to him while my fingers flew, and I would say, "I want to be a productive member of society."

When I showed him pictures in our magazines of crowded American parking lots, I added, "These are the cars of American workers. See the plant over there. They come to work in their own cars." He was indignant and said that he didn't believe it. "Your government puts out those pictures as propaganda, and we won't be fooled by it."

"What do you think about the war in Korea?" he queried. "Why is your Air Force dropping germs on our

Shandung Province?" I professed ignorance about what was going on in Korea and stated that I was sure my country would not engage in germ warfare. "Of course they do," he answered. "It is in all our newspapers."

We continued to spar with one another. He wanted to know what improvements I had noticed taking place in China. I didn't want to give needless offense, but neither did I want to lie. I could honestly commend the politeness of the soldiers and their identification with the needs of the common people. I admired the speed with which the Communists made literature available and emphasized literacy.

My detention faced me with the problem of getting exercise. We had a relatively deep garden running the length of our building and beyond. Also I was able to go through a door in the wall and walk around in the next compound. It wasn't much, but I could make one circuit after another. I had never had so much time to look at the mountains around the city. They towered up so steeply that they added to my sense of confinement. I had lost my freedom around the river valley, but for that matter the citizens of Kangding were not that free to move around within the city. It had been divided into three zones. A person living in one zone was checked before entering another zone. I said to myself, "Chen thinks it is up to him whether we go or stay. He has hinted as much, but I have the upper hand. I know that the moment God wants us to go, we'll go, and nobody can stop us."

Our family in Kangding

In our first energetic flurry of packing and preparing to leave in the summer I had given all my heavy winter under-clothes away. Now I had to beg back a set because it was getting cold enough to wear warm clothing. We had also disposed of a lot of our tinned food stores, and these we had no way of getting back or replacing.

We continued to sort through things we had, looking for ways of disposing of them. We had a surprise request from a Communist cadre to buy our pump organ for his organiza-tion and we sold it to him.

Betty sat down to write her parents, saying, "We had

hoped that we might spend this Christmas with you, but our heavenly Father knows best. I am reminded of the words which were such a blessing to McConkey, 'You can trust the Man who died for you.' There is much comfort and assurance that I long to write of to you. We think of you so much these days, knowing how easily you could be tempted to worry. But it is useless to repeat back to you things we learned from you. Rest assured that the lessons are standing us in good stead. It's equal joy to go or stay."

We had been away from home six years, from 1945 to 1951, and the end was not yet. My father wrote me from the Philippines to tell me that he had not been well and had been having some tests. He said he hoped we would get out of China soon and asked us to route ourselves via the Philippines. "We want to see you," I wrote back, "and we'll come as soon as we can. But right now we're being held up indefinitely."

I added, "God always uses delays profitably if we let him. These months have had their tiring, irritating, boring side, but on the other hand we have been grateful for the opportunity to be patient, for time to reflect, time to wait on God for the future plans he has for us. And we have been thankful for the note of peace and joy we have. God has been stirring all the Christian community to be serious about what is facing us. We aren't living on Easy Street, but that is no occasion for long faces or grumbling."

Losang, a Tibetan trader, came by to see me one day. Over a cup of tea he confided in me, "I can't leave Kangding any more than you can. We Tibetans have lost our freedom too."

"Things have tightened up a lot compared with last spring," I replied.

"So tight that we can't do business," said Losang. "We are being taxed on all goods from India. We were never taxed like this before. Did you hear about the cigarettes?"

"What cigarettes?"

"One of my friends was so disgusted that rather than pay taxes on them, he threw his stock of Indian cigarettes into the river. And when some of the cadres rushed down and tried to fish the bales out, he laughed at them. He'll probably get into trouble for that."

"Well, Losang, I hear that they have stationed observers outside the church to list the names of the people who attend. Remember that when you Buddhists are no longer free to practice your religion!"

"I didn't see anyone outside your gate when I came in here," Losang said with a smile.

"Do you mean to say that you actually looked around to see if there was anybody?" I asked.

He chuckled; then he laughed aloud. "Come to think of it that's what I did," he said. "But we Tibetans look on the bright side. We have a proverb that says, 'Bees can never blow down the king of the mountains with the flapping of their wings.'" And with a wink and a wave of his hand he was gone.

Friends were becoming more and more precious. The day before Christmas Bryce Gray, an Irishman with the CIM, came in carrying a big bag. He had been constructing some gifts for Marion and Teddy and wanted to install one of them. With the children safely out of the way, he drew out a wooden cradle for Marion's doll. Since he was an artist, he had painted a design on the headboard and then varnished the doll bed.

"Oh, she will be ecstatic about that," Betty exclaimed. "I'm glad you came this early because I'll have time to get some bedding ready to fit your cradle."

"I thought and thought about what would be appropriate for each of them, and here's what I made for Teddy," Bryce said. With that he drew out the pieces for a small child's swing. It was enclosed with a back, sides and safety bar at the front. This bar slid up and down on two of the four ropes, one placed at each corner.

"I had to come up early to install this, he explained. "I wanted to have it in place for him to discover on Christmas morning." The swing had a cartoon figure painted on the back and was also varnished. I helped him get the swing attached to the middle of the ceiling where it could easily move forward and backward without touching the walls. The room was so large, and the ceiling so high in our old-fashioned Chinese building that there would be no trouble using the swing inside. We tied up the swing to one wall and covered it so it wasn't apparent what it was. In all my many Christmases I have never seen the equal of Bryce's ingenuity in terms of craftsmanship, as well as his choice gifts for our children.

Marion had never had a doll until Nellie Stokes made one for her. When she received the gift, she hugged it and promptly named the doll, "Moses." Betty tried in vain to get her to change the name. Moses it was, and Moses it would continue to be. We knew she would be so happy to have a place to put Moses to sleep. As for Teddy, well, we could hardly wait to see how he would react to his new swing.

That Christmas of 1950 was remarkable in other ways. Early in the morning an agitated nun rapped on the door and brought us the message that Bishop Valentine had just been taken down to the police station. The other priests were getting ready in case they might be put in prison. He was the senior foreigner in the city.

"Well, how should I get ready just in case I am taken to prison on Christmas Day?" I asked.

"I'll get a bag," Betty said, "You'll want soap, towel and washcloth, toothbrush and toothpaste."

"I'll want my sleeping bag," I added.

"Don't forget you would need to shave. And you probably ought to have a few medicines."

It didn't take long to prepare two small parcels and set them beside the door. Betty then insisted that I dress warmly and have outer garments handy in case there came a peremptory tap at the door.

"All right! All right! Now let's enjoy Christmas," I said. We had a small Christmas tree. We told the nativity story, and then we had songs and prayer. The highlight was when we took Marion and Teddy into the room where we had their gifts. Marion took a moment or so to figure out what the rocking cradle was and then she laid Moses in it and began to rock the doll. As for Teddy, he was thrilled with his rides in the swing. He gurgled and laughed and held on tightly to the bar as we swung him back and forth.

Further news came that George Kraft had been taken to the police station as well as the Bishop but no knocking at our gate for me. By dusk George was released, and the Bishop was held at the police station until late that evening.

"Poor fellow," George reported later, "It was a hard day for both of us because we were forced to stand much of the time. The Bishop is so much older than I am. We were being questioned in separate rooms, and I was asked about all of you. When I left, the interrogators were trying to get the Bishop to implicate his Chinese secretary as a member of the Nationalist party. He kept saying that he knew nothing whatsoever about the secretary's political views. One policeman shouted at him, 'We know he is a party member! Now we have told you, so that you know he is. We want you to write down that you know what party he is working for.' Weary as the Bishop was, he never gave in."

Shortly after Christmas we received word that Geoffrey Bull, having been captured by the military near Chamdo, had arrived in Kangding on his way under escort to prison down-country. When we prepared food and took it to the authorities for him, they refused to accept it, denying that he was in town. But our former cook, Ahnu, was passing the gateway of a military compound and, glancing in, she saw and immediately recognized Geoff. We were so sorry to miss a contact with him, for we knew he was facing some serious charges by the new government.

A few days later our good friend, John Ding, came back to Kangding and confirmed that indeed Geoff had just been escorted under guard toward Chengdu. John had been in the river town of Yajiang on the Batang road around Christmas. One morning he met a Chinese officer who said to him, "I am in charge of taking an Englishman named Bull to prison. Do you know him? I can let you talk to him." John asked to meet Geoff and talked briefly with him about his capture, detention in Batang, and current trip to prison. "I'm all right except for the spicy food I get," Geoff reported. "These Sichuanese like it terribly hot, too hot for me!"

One freezing day in February 1951 my interrogator, Chen, came at his usual time but on a different mission. "Your applications to leave Kangding have been approved," he announced. "Six adults and two children. As far as we are concerned, you are permitted to go out around town now and make preparations. The requirement is that each foreign adult must post notices of departure so that if anyone has a debt to collect or an accusation to make he can do so. You will also have to find individual guarantors to sign for each one of you. These guarantors must be responsible citizens with some property or business. You will also have to leave all properties of your organization and find someone responsible for keeping them. Then your travel arrange-ments are up to you. Get your own transport. You may only take personal possessions with you. You will go as far as Yaan and report at the Foreign Affairs Office there. That office issues your exit permits for the remainder of your journey to Hong Kong. You must leave here within five days of this notice."

When he had left, we tried to digest the news. I said to

Betty, "I can get out at last! I really think that Chen enjoyed telling us how many requirements we have to fulfill in order to leave. It is like so many hoops through which we have to jump. We're going to be very busy the next five days!"

The other foreigners who were waiting for permission to leave welcomed this break in the logjam. They were ready to assist in getting us ready if they could. An elderly Chinese scholar wrote out our departure posters with a brush pen, eight for each of us, 48 all together. I was to report at the police station with my roll of posters and my own paste. Betty made a pot of flour paste for me. A surly policeman led me around, pointed out locations, and waited impatiently as I stuck the floppy notices up on the rough walls around the city. Some of my fingers were bleeding by the time I got through, for some of the surfaces had sharp points sticking out to catch the unwary.

I hoped the posters wouldn't spark any trouble for us, and no one complained. Earlier one of Mako's sisters had made an accusation that we had forced her brother to marry Lozongdrema. Fortunately, he repudiated that, and it went no further.

A friend accepted responsibility for the furniture and other mission property that we had to leave in storage. Transport this trip would no longer be by chair since the Communists had outlawed such demeaning human labor. The best we could find were pack animals with wooden saddles. We already had rice baskets with seats in them for the children to ride in. Carriers could sling these baskets on their shoulders without breaking the law. The matter of guarantors was more complicated. Who would want to risk his name and property by guaranteeing a foreigner? John Ding for one. But with my most industrious efforts I only secured two more. Three of the ladies were without guarantors. As the time drew near for us to go, I told Chen that I could do no more than that. "Oh," he said airily, "It doesn't matter; the other three can leave anyway." I breathed deeply and reined in my exasperation as I thought of the fruitless hours I had spent searching for more guarantors.

We were up until three o'clock the night before we left. It was a very tired crew that filed out the next morning. A number of local Christians were among those who saw us off at the city gate. "We are your brothers and sisters," they told us, "We wish you God's blessing and hope you come back some day. We'll be here to greet you on your return."

We tucked blankets around the children in their baskets. "I'm afraid Marion is going to find the bottom too tights for her feet," Betty said, "She's grown so much in the seven months since we designed those seats to fit them."

The guards had examined our papers and had searched us. They motioned that we were free to go. We said our farewells to our friends and I started down the road on foot, following the children. The five ladies perched precariously on bed-rolls on their lumbering pack animals. The roar of the river was deafening as always, and we collected our thoughts while occasionally signaling to one another at a striking view or a swinging bridge.

CHAPTER 24

A ROUGH PASSAGE SMOOTHED

As I swung down the road behind the porters carrying Marion and Teddy I had an indescribable sense of freedom. It was March, 1951, and six years had passed since we had sailed from Philadelphia on our way to Kham. Now we were starting on the way back home. True we did not have official papers to travel farther than Yaan, but it was good to be underway after waiting seven months.

At Luding we crossed the old chain bridge. That night our inn was an unusually miserable shack with a dirt floor, wobbly beds, and walls that did not reach up to the eaves. Marion cocked her head and asked, "Mummy, is this home?" Betty wearily replied, "It's home for tonight, dear."

Up and over Two Wolf Mountain we encountered lots of snow, to be expected in March. Those physical conditions were hard, but added to them were continual stops for inspection of our papers and pawing over our meager possessions. Another thing we noticed was the absence of the well-run inns we had been used to. Service had degenerated. People were trying to look poor and act poor, and if that meant leaving the dust and cobwebs, so be it. All along the way we saw swarms of road crews working on the new motor road, most of them forced labor. Once over the pass we found that we could rent two carts, each pulled by three mules. We decided to make the change. These carts were two-wheeled but had rubber tires. As we sat on the hard planks and bumped along, we found that a cart had drawbacks. The squeal of the wheels for hours on end was excruciating to the ears. But we had the children on our laps, and they were happy with the sights. We saw farmers at work in the fields. It was slow going, and we were glad to jump off the second day at the Yaan Bridge. I hired carriers for our baggage, and then we pushed and shoved through the crowds on the bridge and the main street. In the midst of this packed scene, I spotted an old friend from Ganzi. Mingma was smiling broadly as he recognized me, and I smiled back. We had a brief greeting, and then he was gone. It would be my last sight of a Khamba Tibetan for a while. Eighteen Khambas had confessed faith in Christ during our team's brief ministry, and we knew they would face much testing in the days ahead.

Our party in Yaan was collecting such a flock of curious people around us that we finally stopped in a tea shop. There we took possession of a corner, fended off the crowd which had followed us in, and I went on by myself to the police station. We had taken for granted that, after checking in, we could stay as usual at the home of our friends, Dr. and Mrs. Crook. The official told me curtly that we would not be allowed to stay with other foreigners. But then where? In answer he scribbled an address on a piece of paper and told me that this was where we were assigned to stay. I backtracked until I reached the tea shop, and we all went to the place listed on the paper. The man who opened the door refused us entrance. Back we threaded our way to the tea shop, and I returned to the police station to explain we had a problem. The officer was furious. He said, "Tell the people there they have to take you. It's a police order. Look, I'll send a policeman with you."

For the fourth time we trailed along the street, six of us, two children and the porters. I hammered on the door, and when the same man opened it, I pushed my way in. The policeman explained that it was a police order that we lodge at this place. The man finally nodded his head and pointed us to the passageway beyond the shop front. Once our load carriers had come in the main door, he slammed it shut in the faces of the fascinated crowd. He led us up a flight of stairs and showed us to two rooms, one large and one small. "You ladies take the large room," I said. "Our family can manage in the small room." We counted our pieces of luggage and I paid off the carriers. At that point it was great to sink down on some board beds and just rest a while.

We were mystified at this so-called "inn." At the front it was a shop selling oil for lamps. And yet it was obvious that the place had some rooms at the back for travelers. Why were we so unwelcome? The building was in dreadful disrepair. Our windows were missing most of their panes of glass, and mosquitoes were humming around. We saw a lot of broken glass on the floor. After one night we knew that the house was alive with rats. Our room had thirteen rat holes. We were glad that since there were two beds, we could each sleep with one of the children. I experimented with stopping up the rat holes with broken pieces of glass, only to discover the next night that I had trapped a rat inside our room. He was industriously making a new hole in order to escape. We placed our food provisions in a small bag hung by a rope across the middle of the room, but in the darkness rats would jump up and perch on the bag, munching through its plastic sides. These Sichuan rats could be the size of a cat. Betty got to recognize one old rat by a scar it bore. It was so fearless that it would scuttle by us on the stairs in daytime. We had heard of children being attacked by rats, so we were especially alert whenever ours were napping.

Room service there was none. Pails of water were hard to come by. And we had to eat in restaurants outside or bring food in. The shop owner's family would hardly speak to us. We had never felt so unwelcome. Of course, we were foreigners, but that wasn't sufficient to explain the cold shoulder we were receiving.

Nor, as days passed, did we understand why we were being held so long in Yaan. On one of our visits to the police station, Betty and I noticed another foreigner while crossing a courtyard. He was sitting over to one side, busily scribbling at a table. When I had made one more unfruitful inquiry about our exit visas, I went over to this man and introduced myself. He was a foreign doctor from a city to the south of us, and at this point he was trying to compose a trite confession for publication in the local newspaper. As he and his wife, and four children, were about to take a bus to Chengdu, he had seated the rest of his family on the bus and was having their luggage inspected. An official picked up a black cylinder of what we used to call "aerosol bombs." Betty and I had often used these in inns to kill bedbugs. The official asked, "What is this?" The doctor had made the mistake of trying a little levity. "Well, I can guarantee that it isn't an atom bomb," he replied. The official, angry at this "insult to the Chinese nation," ordered the family to remain in Yaan until this misdemeanor was punished. Here was the doctor, looking like a boy caught in some mischief, trying to be properly apologetic without compromising his honesty.

Another foreign doctor was in prison in Yaan. He unwisely had had a hobby of taking weather observations, presumably, according to the Communist authorities, for the CIA or the American Air Force. His wife had been living for a long time at an inn in the city, hoping for his release. They even had the grave of a daughter there in Yaan. This dear lady had spent years in this area, had many Chinese friends in Yaan and yet like us was isolated from them. At last she had to leave alone for Hong Kong where she continued her vigil until her husband was finally released from prison and left the country.

We received no explanation for the delay in expelling us from the country. We became familiar with a number of good restaurants; that is, the food was good. The surroundings were another matter. But one day a policeman stopped us on the street and ordered us back to our lodging. "But we are going out to eat," we said. "You had no permission to be on the streets of Yaan," he replied. From that time on we made our forays outside with careful advance sighting up and down the street to be sure no police were in sight.

Meanwhile, our friends in Yaan, the Crooks, were concerned about our welfare. They sent a servant woman over to see us. This woman set down the basket she was carrying, uncovered it, and lifted out food items as well as a selection of books for us to read! She asked us if we had any laundry, which we did, and she took it all. From that time on we looked forward to the daily visits we had from this kindly woman. She thought it great sport to be bringing in goodies for us, and we also wrote letters and received replies from the Crooks. Once when Marion was running a fever, Dr. Crook even got permission to pay her a medical call.

On one occasion Betty heard shrieks from a nearby room. Looking through a crack in the wall, she could see a woman beating a ten-year-old girl with a thick stick. The child jumped on and off a bed, trying to avoid the blows, and she finally dashed out into the hall. Betty went out and restrained the woman, who was trembling with anger. Chinese readily accept this type of intercession and halting of an altercation. She may have been the wife of the oil shop's owner. By this time we knew they were both under great stress. Once wealthy, they had been gradually stripped of their possessions. Their servants had departed, and now they feared for their lives. During the weeks that we were there we saw this man lose a great deal of weight, while he was forced to march in parades and shout with others the slogans and songs of the day. While we were there, he was also tortured, being hung by the thumbs right in his own house as the officials kept trying to get him to disgorge his supposedly hidden treasure. No wonder he had tried to bar us from entering his building, because he was so shattered by his hopeless plight.

Marion and Teddy, in their innocence of what was going on, enjoyed watching the youth meetings which took place in a vacant lot right under our window. "Chang, chang...chang, chang, chang," the crowd would sing over and over and Marion would repeat this. The boys and girls down below began to teach her their songs and thought it was a great joke for a foreign child to be singing their new songs. We thought this was going a little too far, but the only way we could check it was to keep her away from the window. Easier said than done. The chants from outside were so compelling, and she had little else to do than watch the excitement.

In early May a heat wave brought the first flies as well as a rising stench from the toilet pits located below us. This was becoming intolerable. Then the four single ladies received notice of their exit visas while I was told our family would have to continue to wait. How quiet it seemed after they left! A week passed and then another. Now our supply of cash was running out, so I made a trip to the police station. "I want to notify you," I told the officer in charge, "that my family is almost out of money to pay rent and buy food. We have had money sent to a bank here, but we cannot withdraw it. The bank requires us to have a local guarantor of some substance, and we are not acquainted with any such person locally who would be willing to do that for us. Thus, if we continue to be held here in Yaan, we request that you be prepared to provide for our food and lodging."

It worked. Within two days I was told to go to the bus station and get bus tickets to Chengdu. I walked the long distance to the bus station across the river in the sweltering sun only to be told that they would not sell me tickets unless I had a travel document. Back I plodded to the police station. They must have known it all along and perhaps enjoyed sending me off on a fruitless trip. An official wrote out what I needed. The paper stated that we were being given ten days to get out of the country. That seemed impossible. I would probably have to get an extension somewhere along the way, but we were certainly ready to go! I went back to tell Betty and the children. It was May 13, 1951 when we started up again after a two month delay. We had no idea where the "old girls", as we sometimes called them, would be by this time. Anything seemed possible. We might or might not meet them along the way.

When we reached Chengdu, we were stopped at least five times by police inspecting our papers as we crossed the city. Our friend, Sam, at the guest house had news for us. "David," he said, "Come with me immediately. If we can get your application in, you can fly to Chungqing tomorrow. It has been weeks since we have had an opportunity like this." I hastily got our papers and went with him. The next morning we had a trip on a practically empty DC3. We sat strapped in seats along the side, the four of us the only passengers apart from two canaries in a cage! Again in Chungqing a friend of ours told us that he had already arranged for us to go on by plane to Hankow the next day. Such an opportunity was rare, and he didn't want us to miss it. On this second trip by air which followed a course down the river gorges eastward all seats were filled. Up in the sky we were buffeted by a windstorm. Rain dashed against the windows, and we could see little outside. A friendly Russian officer seated in front of us reached around and gave Marion and Teddy some candy. They were thrilled and munched on it happily. But many of the passengers were violently sick from the jolting of the plane. As we approached Hankow we ran out of the storm and circled to land.

As Betty said in the airport building, "I was too scared to be sick. And when we got off I felt like I ought to get down and kiss the ground."

We were south of the Yangtse River with Hankow on the north bank. Holding our children tightly, we scrambled up on a river launch in order to reach the appropriate office where we had to check in. What a jam, but we made it. Next we bought our tickets by train to Guangzhou. What we didn't know was that there is a main station and a second, smaller station in the city. We were taken to the smaller of these two, one from which few passengers left. Shortly before train time officials came around and insisted on examining carefully everything we were carrying. One woman inspector picked up Marion's doll, Moses. "What's in this?" she demanded. Betty was frantic, knowing how attached Marion was to this precious possession. "There's nothing in it but cotton," she told the woman. "Please, my little daughter will cry if anything happens to it." The woman began to feel the head and body of the doll and finally satisfied herself that there was nothing secreted in it. She handed Moses back. I scrambled to get baggage together. There were no porters, so I dragged our bags across the station floor while Betty took the children.

Hearing the whistle of the approaching express, a station employee finally came over, picked up some of the baggage and guided us toward the tracks outside. We had to cross two tracks and climb up on a platform. We could see the light of the oncoming engine heading towards us. We barely made it before our train thundered in. We were pushed into the doorway of the nearest car, and the train began to move again. Later we trailed through the train and found our proper seats, but we'll never forget that final rush. Across the unlighted platform from us were some boxcars, and they had horses in them. As the train rolled in, these horses began to throw themselves around in fright, their hooves beating a tattoo against the side of their cars. We were in darkness except for some light from the coaches. Our conductor was quite surprised when we turned up, and he explained that passengers usually joined the train at the main riverside station. We realized then that we had been steered to the wrong station. The last straw was that I couldn't find my tickets. The conductor understood my confusion and kindly said, "I'll come back later."

While this was going on, Marion, with Moses safely in her arms, sat utterly contented. Teddy was sound asleep in a corner. Betty and I looked at each other. "That was a nightmare," I said, "I can't believe it. If that man hadn't helped us get to the platform, we never would have made it."

"As we were crossing those tracks," she commented, "that engine headlight seemed so near, I was afraid that we were going to be hit. Those cement steps were so steep! Well! We made it!" We settled down, and I located the missing tickets. We needed the next two days on the train to rest up. Even then Kuangzhou and Canton were a bit of a blur except for the faded glory of the hotel dining room. It seemed so incongruous to sit down at a table with a snowy white tablecloth and large white napkins. To have a silver-plated cover on the butter dish and finger bowls, while all the while we were surrounded by Communist egalitarianism.

The next day, only the eighth since leaving Yaan, we reached the Hong Kong border. We were met by Margaret's sister, Lillian, and to our surprise she informed us we had arrived ahead of the single ladies! They were slowed down by going by steamer down the Yangtze River. As we got on the sparkling clean train for Hong Kong, she brought out candy bars for the children. At one of the way stations, another train had stopped, going the other direction. The car opposite was filled with British soldiers. Marion was watching them intently. But their train started and they disappeared. At that she broke into tears. "Where have all the uncles gone?" she sobbed. The "aunties" had disappeared from our rooms in Yaan, and now these "uncles" (as she called western men) were leaving. It was too much for her to understand, and we couldn't explain to her that one of these days, things would get back to normal.

For all of us the big city of Hong Kong was confusing. We found ourselves experiencing culture shock because of the well-dressed crowds and the constant roar of traffic. I had come out of China wearing a pair of black cloth shoes. We had managed to bring out a colorful set of Tibetan saddle blankets and some other artifacts, and they were in one corner of our hotel room. On the other side we had our purchases of new clothing. We could hardly bear to throw away the attractive store bags we were accumulating.

In the dining room of our hotel a foreign professor who had come out from Hankow said to me bitterly, "I thought the new government would want my expertise and that I could stay on in China. I was wrong. Their motto right now is 'Destroy; then build!' And they don't want us around for any of the buildup of their new China."

Yes, I could understand that, but my thoughts were elsewhere. What was it that Miss Wang in her plain blue gowns had said to us as we left the Tibetan border? She had said, "We'll carry on until you come back." These members of one of the original Back to Jerusalem Bands would not be leaving. And we came back years later on a visit to rejoice with them in what God had done among Tibetans in our absence.

CHAPTER 25

GOD'S WAY TO FREEDOM

Some years later in Taipei, Taiwan, where we were stationed with TEAM Mission, our living room was crowded with Tibetans who had come to meet and listen to Eliyah Phuntsok from India. Half of the westerners from Kham had relocated in Taiwan and Hong Kong while half had moved over to Tibetan work in India. Phuntsok, who came from Ladakh in Kashmir, said to the group of Tibetan refugees from mainland China, "I was taught the Buddhist philosophy of rebirth and Karma. I used to prostrate myself before the idols a hundred times daily and recite the prayers a thousand times. One day the Rev. Yoseb Gergan, who translated God's Word into our Tibetan language, gave me a booklet telling of the most remarkable transformations as sinners were saved by believing in Jesus Christ. It showed me so simply the redeeming love of Jesus that I received great conviction of sin and my need of a Savior. At last the love of Jesus laid its powerful grasp on my soul. I accepted Jesus as my Savior. Christianity cannot be compared. It can only be contrasted. It is a revelation from God himself, preached by God himself in Christ."

He proceeded to tell of the tremendous changes and

blessing God had brought into his life. I heard similar testimonies from other Tibetans on my many visits to India, which TEAM sponsored. The lama Chekub was finally brought into freedom by a vision of Christ. Then as a Christian evangelist, he saw an impoverished Indian woman during a famine, who was preparing to toss her infant son into a river. He saved the baby boy, took him home to his wife, and they raised him as their own. I also sat across from a Tibetan pastor evangelist, Peter Rapgey, in Darjeeling as he told me his story: "For seven years, I was under the tutelage of a lama in Kalimpong, but then he became sick and was close to death. He asked me to call the Christian pastor, Tharchin, to his bedside. When I returned with the pastor, to my surprise my mentor lama asked him to take me home with him, saying, 'I don't want to have Rapgey left here in this monastery when I die. Will you take him and train him in the ways of your Jesus?' And Pastor Tharchin gladly accepted me. And what joy I found in Jesus, and with what joy I share the knowledge of him with other Tibetans in Sikkim, Nepal, and even Bhutan."

In regard to those whom we had known in China we had heard that Lucille Chang had been forced to work in a factory in Shanghai. I visualized her at her machine, saying to herself as she worked, "For Jesus, for Jesus," as well as being a blessing to her coworkers. In later years she was able to visit her daughter, Anna Louise, in Hong Kong, but returning to Soochow died close to the time one of her sisters died in prison.

Phillip, who had helped us on our trip into Batang, has been for years a church planter in Assam, India. It is amazing to realize that he can pick up a phone and call his family members back in Batang. He has been able to lead two relatives who came out to India to faith in Jesus.

John Ding spent 22 years in prison and labor camp. His wife, I-ming, was imprisoned also, and they met but once.

Both transferred to another prison, where she died, though he was not informed of this for three years. He was told that he could not find her grave. When her possessions were brought to him, they were just a gown worn out at the knees from prayer and a quilt in good condition. This latter, he was glad to have because his own was in tatters. John had been imprisoned with about thirty Tibetan men, many of them with lice in their braided hair. When they were told by authorities that their long braids of hair were going to be cut off, they were furious until John calmed them down, saying, "I am a barber. Let me cut your braids off, put your prison number on each one. Then when you are released, you can attach your braid to your head until fresh hair grows out." That settled the problem. Another day in the prison mess hall, after he prayed thanks over his food tray, he found when he opened his eyes that someone had taken it away. The men around him scoffed at him, but he simply said, "If God wants me to eat today, I'll eat. And if not, I just won't eat." The others ate and left, but he sat in his place quietly. Then a cook came out of the kitchen, breaking prison rules, and brought him another plate of food. So he had his dinner after all! God continued to bless and use him in prison. Years later when released, at great risk he resumed his preaching in many parts of China. Eventually he was allowed to come to the United States where he remained till he died in his 80's.

Mako, according to John Ding, returned to Kangding where he was outstanding for his faithfulness and fearlessness among the Christians. Wangden continued his work in Ganzi until he was brutally murdered by a drunk fellow Tibetan. A Han Chinese couple soon volunteered and went up to Ganzi to take his place, but then they were imprisoned for a long time. Elder Wang, a tea merchant, also in Kangding, early on had decided to get Bible school training while it was still available, then returned to Kangding to serve as a pastor all the years up to the present. We met him and his wife, and Miss Wang, who had also survived and continued her ministry, on our visit to Kangding. A portion of the former chapel had been moved and reconstructed elsewhere, and there we attended a service. Lately a completely new church building has been erected. The congregation has sent some Tibetans for training for ministry, and the local Catholics in the city have a Tibetan priest.

As to other changes, the former CIM duplex was destroyed by an earthquake. Our former house has been turned into a boys' dormitory at a school for Tibetans. The students welcomed us to walk through the familiar rooms, still with their high wooden sills in the doorways. The garden was now a sports field, and we were glad that all this is being put to such a good use.

When we visited the city of Lhasa, we met with university students, and I talked with one primary school teacher elsewhere. Later on our return plane trip to Chengdu a large number of joyous and scruffy-looking Tibetan boys were aboard, chosen and sent by the Chinese government for further education. We reflected on the new life awaiting them "down country" as well as the changes taking place in Tibet. It was losing its isolation. Monastic political power had disappeared. A middle class is developing, and perhaps more significantly Tibetans are impressed by the Dalai Lama moving around fully at ease in the modern world. He has put a blessing on education and rapid transportation. Once the railway is completed from the northeast to Lhasa, Tibet will become increasingly accessible and so will "down country" provinces be to Tibetans. Already Tibetans in large numbers have settled in India as well as other parts of the world. The number of well-educated Tibetans in positions of leadership around the Dalai Lama is growing. This type of change has not been forced on them. It is something they themselves have sought for and welcomed. Somewhat like the Armenians, they have not lost their solidarity or identity in spite of being outside Tibet.

Tibetan Buddhism and Buddhism in general are being tested at the practical level of what they offer in satisfaction and life transformation. This is where Christian faith has the power to attract and appeal. Let me give an example.

At one time Betty and I were living in a third floor apartment of a new building in Kowloon, Hong Kong. We began to wonder why billows of wood smoke drifted up into our kitchen area as well as incense up the stairwell. The landlord's family lived below us, and I became a friend of his eldest son, a practicing Christian. The other members of the family were Buddhists, and he told me the secret of the smoke. Three years previously his father had become ill, and Buddhist priests, when called, declared that this was due to the bad luck of the large private house and garden where they were then living. They told the father to sell, even at a loss and get out of the house. They also, with a fee as usual, guided him to a plot of land in Kowloon where a building according to them would be propitious. They "cleansed" the lot for a fee, and presided over a final topping off of the finished building – for a fee. Then when the landlord was going to move in, they told him it would be unlucky for him to use both right and left apartments on the second floor. He then consented to move the nine family members into one two bedroom apartment. And when he was going to move in his electric range, they informed him that he must not use either electricity or gas to cook with. He must use only wood fires. So here was the reason we were experiencing wood smoke in our kitchen and incense up the stairwell. This was in modern Hong Kong where I was working on a Christian magazine in Chinese, which was selling on the local newsstands. I supplied copies of this as well as other literature for my friend, the landlord's son, to leave around his home below us for his family to read.

This situation reminded us of Tibet and the bondage there that had kept sick patients away from our dispensary. Even as that landlord's son continued to pray for the release of his family from bondage, so there is a massive amount of prayer being lifted to God in China in behalf of others, prayer that his will be done on earth for them as it is in heaven! And that loving prayer includes their Tibetan brothers and sisters.

A Han Chinese Christian deeply involved in witness to Tibetans has said with joy that some Tibetan Christians with enthusiasm for the same gospel work are helped to get Bible training so that they can join together in continued outreach to Tibetans. They give the message of assurance possible in this life by the possession of eternal life through Christ. Theirs is the opportunity to exercise the typical Tibetan hospitality (that so often says, "Have a cup of Tibetan tea!"), followed by a chat leading up to Jesus.

Printed in the United States
45509LVS00002B/403-450